"PURE RELIGION" COMES ALIVE

DONALD W. TODD

DEDICATION

It is an honor to dedicate this book to

Dick and Carolyn Apple.

From the earliest days of our inner-city mission

in Memphis, they have been a tremendous

blessing to us in so many ways.

Their sacrifice and unselfishness

have truly inspired us through many challenges.

For all these years

we have been pleased to call them: "friends."

Our world needs more people

just like them.

ACKNOWLEDGEMENT

If not for the love of God, my precious heavenly Father,

and His Son, Jesus Christ,

where would I be? Where would any of us be?

My recent activities and events have come out of His love for me.

He has made me so much more aware of His Presence,

The Holy Spirit, with me and within me.

On my own, I would never have the concern for others,

especially the very poor, that He wants me to have.

He put within me His own Spirit,

the Spirit of truth,

and the Spirit of love.

This book, I believe, is a result of His love

shown to me, undeserving as I am.

May He bless you,

as He has blessed me.

CONTENTS

FOREWORD

In <u>Pure Religion</u> Don writes, "It's something powerfully spiritual when the Holy Spirit touches your heart with something radically different from anything you have ever done before. When we say, 'Yes' to the Spirit's leading, all the resources of heaven are at our disposal." Here Don identifies and defines the origin and wellspring of pure religion.

Mother Teresa received the Nobel Peace Prize for simply living as every Christian should live. On one occasion, when she was given a bag of rice, she asked for her assistant and said, "Take a third of this to Eshaal and a third to Dharma," two ladies who lived on her street … one a Muslim and the other a Hindu. This is pure religion.

<u>Pure religion disturbs people. It involves allowing God to take you off the spiritual throne in the control room of your heart and will, and place Christ on the throne.</u> We no longer make common-sense decisions and ask God to bless them. Rather, we think with the mind of Christ and react in the way we see Him respond in the Gospels.

Fulton J. Sheen was asked to pray for a man so ravished with leprosy that he could not stand. When Sheen bent over him to pray, the cross hanging from his neck fell into an open sore on the man's chest. At that split second Sheen realized that God was "connecting the dots"

… that the cross in the wound was pure religion.

Don points out that we will not be judged by how much we did for Christ, but by what we surrendered to Him and for what we valued most. Pure religion is to love people and use things, not vice versa. This transformed "a son of thunder" into the "the apostle John." And it will transform us … not day by day, but minute by minute. The clock is ticking!

If the world could somehow identify the power of the church, they would destroy it. But they cannot comprehend the concept of pure religion without the blessed Holy Spirit filling every chamber of the heart … and neither can we. **When Christ controls the throne of our hearts, we will develop a strong family likeness. Pure religion is the cause; my service is the effect.**

Joe Garman, President

American Rehabilitation Ministries

INTRODUCTION

My goal in this book is at least two-fold: first, to give glory to God, and to inspire all who read it to be encouraged, encouraged to allow Him to set you free to live a joyous life in worship and service to Him.

Why is this so important? I am convinced that many, many people are literally stuck in some kind of prison, a prison that is a result of a very legalistic attitude, and a lack of confidence in our ability to actually be Jesus in the world today.

This book I intended to show you how much God wants to set you free! He wants you to be aware of His presence in everything you do. **He wants us to see His grace and His goodness toward us, especially when we have failed, sometimes miserably.** He wants us to truly be aware of our ability to lift others' spirits and to be a blessing to people, many who have failed, are hurting, and who may have given up on life. As long as we are still breathing, there is hope!

In our twenty-first century living, we seem to be terribly distracted and disappointed in our lives. We're trying to keep up with new technologies and trends. We feel left behind, even intimidated, by a new generation. **This book is written to help you bridge that gap and to know you are still relevant. God is not done with you yet.** Change is hard! But it is also constant. God promises to give us all the help we will need to make a difference in our lives. He knows how we feel. He is not disappointed in us!

Our God will help us to find our way back to closeness to Him. If we think maybe He doesn't even like us, we will not have the confidence to venture into new and challenging areas of worship and service. Without His help, we would not know the joy and confidence of being a blessing to others.

The Lord is ready to marshal all of heaven's forces to assist us in getting started: The love of Christ in our hearts; and, the Holy Spirit within us as our Teacher, Counselor, and Guide.

No, it will not always be easy. However, has anything we have ever accomplished been easy? Nothing can take the place of knowing that I have heard God's voice, the Holy Spirit, speaking to me, and that I have responded affirmatively. That is what will bring glory to God, and take us into the world of loving, caring for, and serving others, in His Name. **Pure Religion: try it, you will love it!**

CHAPTER 1

DID GOD SET ME UP?

James 1:27 (AV)
Pure religion and undefiled before God and the Father is this, To visit the fatherless and widows in their affliction, and to keep himself unspotted from the world.

IS THIS WHAT "PURE RELIGION" MEANS?

Was I in for yet another culture shock? This wasn't my first third-world mission trip. We were driving through the barren, drought stricken, dirt streets on the outskirts of Lusaka, Zambia, a city of near four million people. Temperature in November, 95 degrees. Our destination: the Chawama community, where we would visit with 50-75 orphaned and abandoned kids, being cared for by perhaps a dozen adults, some of whom were parents, all were women. We arrived in joyous fanfare of excited kids, mainly because my friend, Evangelist A.C. Mutale, had already been visiting and serving this community with food, medicine, and the "Good News," demonstrating Jesus' love for them.

What a joy to be with such a happy group of children. We were taking pictures, giving high-fives, laughing, as if everything was normal. Never mind that they were desperately in need of food, clothing, medicine, hope. Their lives will be much shorter and painful than most people I know. Then, I was asked to sit down and listen as some of the adults began to describe their on-going, desperate, daily urgent needs of caring for so many children. "We have no school, no jobs, and no future for these children." And then, looking directly into my eyes, they said, "Will you help us?" **I don't ever remember being challenged so directly and personally as to whether my faith was genuine - or not.**

IT'S A LONG WAY FROM OKLAHOMA

How well I remember when I was 7 or 8 years old and what it meant when someone very important came to our community. Especially when they actually came to our house. In our own way we were also desperate for help. I was the last of eleven kids, living in the community of Nashoba, deep in the Kiamichi Mountains of Southeast Oklahoma. As a child, I had a very serious problem with my eyes. Normal daily sunlight caused constant, extreme watering and irritation in my eyes. Mama knew it was urgent that I get my eyes examined. Mama (Emily Cent) was 16 years old and living in Paris, France, when, in 1919, she met and married Daddy, an American soldier serving in France during WW 1. He would very soon be sent back to his home in Oklahoma by the U.S. Army, along with his new bride. Upon arriving in the U.S., they began a family that would eventually include nine boys and two girls. Literally, from Paris to poverty, she adapted to her new life in the United States. I cannot imagine the challenges she faced, raising eleven children during very difficult times in our country. Mama would not see her Mama for 27 years. It took intervention from Eleanor Roosevelt to obtain a visa for Grand'Mere to finally come to the U.S. She had 11 grandchildren she had never met. Mama had conquered so many difficulties. But what would she do for me, to save my eyes?

Seems like a pretty small thing compared to what she had already accomplished! Still, it was yet another challenge.

WHAT DID MAMA LEARN IN PARIS THAT I DIDN'T KNOW - YET?

Mama did not lack boldness, and faith, believing that God was in control of this family. At age 12, her father, a successful businessman, mysteriously disappeared. He was never heard from again. Someone suggested that since he was a businessman, perhaps the Nazis, who were invading France, may have kidnaped him in order to seize his wealth. She and her mother, our Grand'Mere, were both devout Catholics where they learned spiritual discipline. Now they had to make it on their own, working hard and trusting God for His protection and provision. It seems that Mama's faith in God as a teenager, led to the very unusual and incredible life that was just ahead for her. In our small Nashoba church, she made sure that all of us were always in church services - every time the doors were open. So, one Sunday, she boldly asked our Missionary / Minister, Harold Dunson, "would you please take Don to get his eyes examined?" We never had a car or any means of transportation to get my eyes examined. This was not a simple request as it would require brother Dunson coming to get me, at three a.m., and taking me to another town several hours drive from where we lived for an eye exam. Since we had no road good enough to get to our house, it meant that he would have to park well over a mile away, then walk, with a flashlight, on a very narrow trail through forest and fields to get me, walk me to his car, then drive for hours for my appointment. We probably went to Hugo, or maybe Durant.

I was known as "the bashful one" in our family, one of the world's worst introverts, rarely speaking more than a few words to anyone outside my own family. It must have been quite a challenge for brother Dunson to spend over 12 hours with me as company. I cannot remember anything we talked about that day. However, I do vividly recall that after we finished the eye exam, we went to a very nice restaurant for lunch. Since my eyes had been dilated, for the first time ever, everything was a blur, including the lunch menu. Embarrassed, I just said, "I guess I'll have what he's having", which was a full adult meal.

Although I was not an orphan and Mama was not a widow, the principle was the same. We were being cared for by someone who cared for others. He treated us like we were his own family. Never complained. Never asked to be paid. He had moved his family from a successful ministry in Garrett, Indiana, to come to our community as a missionary (which means unpaid, raising his own salary) to establish a New Testament church in our community. Harold Dunson, a former Army Chaplain and war veteran, did so many things, good deeds, in his 12-year ministry with us that when he left, he was regarded as one of the most humble and respected men you would ever meet. Hardened men, in the Nashoba community, who had resisted brother Dunson's invitation for years, to come to Christ, were now coming to him to be baptized into Christ before he was gone. He had demonstrated Pure Religion. Since I was so well taught about humility and servanthood, learning from the example of brother Dunson, and others like him, what would I now say to the desperate Zambians pleading, "Will you help us?"

I'VE GOT IT HARD? COMPARED TO WHAT?

This had already been one of the most challenging and difficult foreign mission trips I had ever taken. Brother Mutale had requested that, if possible, I bring 120 King James Bibles. They only use the

KJV. Because of extremely high costs in mailing or shipping these Bibles it meant taking them with me as luggage. With the Bibles, plus a portable baptistry and my own luggage, I now had five bags to check weighing 250 pounds! I thought when I checked the bags in Memphis that they would go directly to Zambia. However, due to my own neglect and not using a travel agent this time, it meant I would have to claim, and re-check, the bags in Chicago. Then, going from the domestic terminal to the international terminal was a sight to see, balancing five bags on a small cart by myself. Arriving in Chicago, Sunday, 8:30 p.m., my next flight was not until 9:30 a.m., thirteen hours away. That meant sleeping on a tile floor as best as I could. After spending $1100.00 on extra luggage fees, I was just glad to finally be on the flight to Africa. I did not share any of this with my new friends in Zambia until much later in the week. Then only to brother Mutale, who was very appreciative and understanding.

THEY ONLY KNOW WHETHER YOU ARE THERE - OR NOT

I have learned that people, especially in poor countries, would not understand what it might take for you or I to get there. Raising thousands of dollars, physical challenges, personal and family commitments. They only know that you are there - or not! Yes, God knows what it takes, and He provides, and blesses, all the way to wherever He is sending you! Besides, you are only there for a short time before you realize that they are more humble, more spiritual, love the Lord more, and praise Him more than I ever have. So, who is the real winner? Me! I may have come to serve and to be a blessing to them. But I am the one being served - and blessed! So, I am not about to start complaining and talking about making sacrifices just to be there.

When the Zambian women finished their very passionate pleas for help, I stood up and responded. "I am so very happy to be here with you, and to spend this special time with you. As to your request that I help you, I am only human, like you. I had to ask people for money to help me come here. I don't have the kind of money you need to do what you ask. But God does. We know that God can do anything. Here's what I promise you I will do. First, I will pray for God to supply your needs. He knows everything. He knows your needs and cares very much for you. Then, when I get back home, I will tell others about you and what you need. And I will ask if anyone joins me in doing what we can to help you."

I'D BETTER MEAN IT

They were very pleased to hear what I had said. It truly came from the heart and with the belief that He would hear and answer my prayers for these people. Before I returned to the U.S., I left financial donations for both communities of orphans as well as for the handicapped seniors center, and for brother Mutale to help carry on his outreach ministries. He literally walks miles, every day, to go and help those most in need. And I made a commitment to send monthly support as God provides. I intend to make this urgent need a challenge to others to help as well. All of Africa? No. But when God reveals a specific, urgent need, how can I say no? Especially when he, the Holy Spirit, not only put me up to it, he says that He's the one Who will do it. Not me. But through me. In the evening we visited a second group of orphans in the Kamwala community whose needs were almost identical as those in the Chawama community. As I listened to their pleas, I made the same commitment to them that I would pray, give, invite others to help, and trust God to supply their needs. That's how Pure Religion works.

WOULD THE HOLY SPIRIT LIE TO ME?

No, but He will "set me up!" I love it! He has every right to. Sometimes it's the only way He can get us where we need to be. What had I learned so far in my first few days in Zambia? Clearly, pray first - about everything! And, next time, use my travel agent! Lord, is it your will? Are you sending me to Zambia, or is it my idea? Do I trust you, Lord, to provide everything I will need? After all, I'll be eighty years old in little over a year. Will you be giving me the energy I will need for such a long trip? Holy Spirit, are you going to use me to be Jesus to these precious people of Africa? I've never been to Zambia before. (Been to Kenya three times) Will they listen to me? Am I ready to gladly give You the glory, Lord? Not glorifying myself? Will I praise you - more than I complain about my "Sacrifices?" Most importantly, will I demonstrate "Pure Religion"? It's a start!

"When we extend mercy to the broken, we reach out with the hands of Christ Himself."

Philip Yancey - **Prayer: Does It Make Any Difference?** (110 - 112)

"Taking the very nature of a servant, being made in human likeness." Philippians 2:7 (NIV)

Lord Jesus, help me to love and serve others as You have loved and served me. May I emulate Your thoughts and attitudes and bring glory to God, our Father. In Your Name. Amen

SOMETHING TO THINK ABOUT:

Does the idea of "Pure Religion" seem impossible to you?

CHAPTER 2

IS SOMETHING MISSING? NO, SOMEONE IS MISSING!

John 16:13-14 NIV

But when he, the Spirit of truth, comes, he will guide you into all truth. He will not speak on his own; he will speak only what he hears, and he will tell you what is yet to come.

14 He will bring glory to me by taking from what is mine and making it known to you.

DO WE KNOW WHO HE REALLY IS?

It is the Holy Spirit Who reveals Jesus, Who He is. It is the holy Spirit Who reveals God, the Father. Who He is. It is the Holy Spirit Who reveals and unveils to us the Word of God, the Holy Scriptures. So how can we possible manage to know what God's will is without the presence and working of the Holy Spirit? And yet, how many times have we not only not invited the Holy Spirit into our situations for immediate wisdom, truth, and guidance, but we have ignored Him as though He did not exist, except in some mystical, hard to understand, ghostly presence? God, the Father does not do anything except through Jesus. Jesus does not do anything other than what is the Father's will, and, He does not do or say anything other than through the Holy Spirit. The Holy Spirit does not do anything other than what He hears from Jesus. And the Holy Spirit does not do anything that is inconsistent with the Written Word of God. Seriously, isn't it time that we began to consult the Holy Spirit (of the living God) before diving into very serious matters affecting the Body of Christ? Things that will have to do with how and why we have gotten so far off course. Such as: Pure Religion (a sincere interest and involvement with the poorest among us); prioritizing our personal and church resources (How are we spending our money and our time?); What is genuine, personal, worship "In Spirit and in truth?"; and dealing with urgent current issues. What I, and many others suspect, is that we prefer to cling to our pre-conceived beliefs and ideas of what the church should be and how everyone else should also agree with us. Yes, please stay true to the Word of God. Stay true to your convictions. But can we not have the kind of love that Jesus had that did not turn away true seekers? We make new friends until we find out that they go to a different church. And that they are not going to leave their church to come to ours. In which case we have no more obligation to befriend them. Certainly not be seen working along-side or worshiping with them, non-believers that they are. If my beliefs and my faith do not stand to be tested, then what do I really have? **The kind of faith that trusts the Holy Spirit will guide us into all truth that allows us to continue to grow in grace and truth**. I think that some may be of the opinion and notion that, if we are sure that we have the correct doctrine (more than anyone else), that nothing else really matters. Big mistake! I just want us to understand who the Holy Spirit is, and that we cannot do without Him. He is the author of Pure Religion.

DO I HAVE A GOOD REASON FOR DOING THIS?

Seriously, I never wanted to write another book. You can ask my wife. So why am I doing it? What God has done for me, what Jesus means to me, what the Holy Spirit is telling me is, "Write this book!" I'm writing this book to encourage you the, perhaps, discouraged reader. Bear with me. I'm not expecting anyone to say, "Wow! What a great writer!" It will probably be just the opposite. My ultimate goal is to bring glory to God, our heavenly Father. I best do this by my living, my giving, and my desire to be just like Jesus. I am only to God what I am to the least of His children. All of whom are created in His glorious image. Then, in Christ, through the indwelling Holy spirit, I become His instrument to influence the world around me to know who they are meant to be in Him, and to know who God is by seeing the life of Christ in me.

DO I HAVE TO GO TO CHURCH?

I meet so many people who are discouraged and disillusioned. Some whose faith has been shattered, unnecessarily, by spiritual leaders, so called, and church members who seem to have little or no humility or Christlikeness. The other day while at the doctor's office, I met a new nurse at the facility. We began to connect as we both agreed that God is good, and we both have been blessed! I love these conversations. Soon, she shared with me that she, her husband and family had in recent years left their long-standing church family to begin their own house church with neighbors and friends. She shared how they no longer felt that they were being fed spiritually. And that they needed a deeper walk with the Lord. Something they said was missing in their local church and denomination.

Now, you and I know that, first, we are commanded "not to forsake the assembling of ourselves together". We also know that some people just don't want to try to fit in and be a part of a church family, with who-knows-what kind of people! But you and I also know that a great many churches, perhaps a majority, care little about anything but going through the motions and keeping things as they have always been. Don't go overtime! Don't rock the boat! Certainly, don't get out of the boat! **So, is it not time to make a statement by making the decision to please God rather than men (or women)?** I am not suggestion that there aren't a lot of great churches that certainly do much more than just meet and eat! Thank God for true disciples who are Jesus in the world today.

DO WE KNOW WHAT'S REALLY GOING ON?

Would you agree, something has gone terribly wrong in many churches, especially in the U. S.? Would you also agree that it might have more to do with negative impressions coming out of our churches that turns people off, rather than the name, or even the doctrines being taught? Is it possible that we can be so "right" that it does more damage than it helps? Is it possible that many churches have totally different priorities than what our Lord does?

Current surveys and polls indicate that there is a serious falling away of the younger generation. Many of them say that the Bible is no longer relevant. That churches are too old fashioned. That no one really cares about or understands them. Is it possible that in the past several decades that we have become so sensitive and self-centered that we adults don't want to offend our kids or grand kids, shutting down lines of communication? And could it be that this current generation has been so conditioned to wanting what they want that the notion of giving, or even sacrificing, for the benefit of others, especially those who don't even deserve to be helped, seems ridiculous? When I speak to groups of juveniles in detention at Juvenile Court the first thing, I do is share my belief that we are all created in the image of God. That He not only made us, but has an individual plan and purpose for each one of us. He even knows everything about us, yet still loves us- unconditionally. **This prepares the way for each one of these teens to see themselves as unique, gifted, loved, and very special in the eyes of God, yet still accountable for their attitudes and actions.** It also gives them hope and encouragement as they look ahead. They have goals and dreams, but also personal challenges and difficulties that have already invaded their young lives, in many cases putting them on a path of self-destruction. Many of them seem ready, with a little encouragement in the right direction, to make a serious change in their lifestyle and behavior, even to the point of accepting Christ as Savior and Lord, and being baptized into Christ.

WHY DO YOU THINK I NEED YOUR HELP?

Why doesn't that seem to work in the hearts and lives of other teens and younger adults? Those who are more affluent and already succeeding in life, with a promising future just ahead. Those who don't have the same hang-ups and problems as the poor or inner-city teens. Probably because we want to be seen as self-sufficient, not dependent on some God who only wants to control our lives. Rebellion comes in different forms, but it is still rebellion. Not just against old-fashioned parents or out of touch churches, but God Himself. **There is still no better guide and no greater need today than to know God and His will.** This is found in the Bible, the Old and New Testaments. God's written Word. Let's not diminish that fact. In all fairness, there are many, many young servants and soldiers of the Lord in the Body of Christ today. It's just that the numbers are dwindling. How can we reverse that?

So, what's going on? And what can be done about it? Can we first look into our own hearts and be honest about how we feel? What frustrates us? What inspires us? Do I feel pressured to act or perform a certain way in ordered to be accepted? Am I willing to put everything on the line in order to get to the bottom of things and to allow the Holy Spirit to be my guide? For me, I dare not criticize anyone else when I first need to look in the mirror, then get into my closet (anywhere I can be totally alone with God) and cry out to God for mercy for a "sinner like me."

WANT TO HEAR ONE "AWESOME" STORY?!

You and I know many stories of people who have become "fed up" with things as they are, churches and church leaders not meeting the needs of the flock. Here is just one such story: Rich Mullins. I won't claim to speak for Rich, certainly not judging him in any way, but simply to take a broad look at one of the most successful and gifted servants of God. Clearly, he used his God-given gifts to bring glory to God. Who doesn't know Rich's songs, "Our God Is An Awesome God!?" Or "Step by Step?" Just some of the great songs penned by Rich Mullins, and to this day sung and heard all over the world. I never shared the stage with Rich, but our concert paths crossed many times in the 1970s. Once I was in a small Indiana town for a church concert when a very nice lady came up to me and introduced herself. "I'm Rich Mullins mother." I was honored, and blessed, to get to know her. I could tell that she was so proud of her son who grew up in a small church in a small town.

According to Wikipedia, Rich Mullins, October 21, 1955 - September 19, 1997, died in a car wreck in Illinois. He was seen as an enigma to the Christian music industry. Often barefoot, unshaven, and badly in need of a haircut, Mullins did not look like the average American Gospel singer and writer. Mullins did not consider his music his primary ministry, but rather a means to pay his bills. Instead, his ministry was the way he treated his neighbors, family, enemies, and those outside the church. Taking a vow of poverty, he accepted a small church salary and spent the last years of his life on a Navajo reservation teaching music to children." Rich overcame whatever challenges he faced to become a huge success in the world of Christian music. And, to leave a legacy that will continue to bless and challenge people for a long time to come**. Are you and I willing to give up everything in search of Pure Religion?**

DOES IT SEEM LIKE SOMETIMES YOU ARE ALL ALONE?

When I started going to minister to Jail East to minister to Juveniles under age 18, being tried as adults, it would be one of the greatest challenges I had ever faced. After all, these had committed very serious crimes. One person helped me and led me into one of the most rewarding times of my ministry. Judy McEwen, now retired a living in Florida, had asked me to be one of the primary Chaplains to these teens. She had won their respect and admiration as she became, to many of them, more loving and influential than their own mother. As they put it. I heard her say to them many times, **"You are not alone. God is always here with you. And I will always be here for you. Don't ever forget that!"** I saw many of these young men weep over their crimes, and in response to the love that Ms. McEwen showed to them. What was really going on? The Holy Spirit, Jesus, was using her to show God's love to them. That He was for them. Not against them. That's what they were really responding to. Now, we know that the promise of God's presence is first and foremost given to those who are His. To those who have accepted Christ as Lord and Savior. Having said that, is it not true that God is always present, ready to answer whenever anyone calls out to Him from the heart? Does He ever say "no"? So, they never are really alone. Unless they chose to ignore Him or those who come in His name. I believe this is a great source of comfort to them, the assurance that God is ready to forgive and accept each and every one into His family.

I have been so blessed to work with some of God's most humble servants in our Juvenile and Jail ministries. I must mention another one in particular. When Judy McEwen retired as Director of Youth Services, she was replaced by Ms. Joyce Anderson who is still the current Director. I have never seen anyone more dedicated to this challenging work than her. From the first day I met her she has inspired me to give my all in this ministry to our youth. She is a model example of someone who truly cares. She demonstrates "Pure Religion".

<u>I believe it is so important for all of us every day to see ourselves as vessels of God's grace and His Presence, the Holy Spirit.</u> What a comfort it would be to others if they felt the Lord's Presence when we show up. Has anyone ever told you, or implied, "I see Jesus in you?" After spending time with you, do people know that God loves them. Does your "faith" draw you closer to "sinners?" I don't want to end a single day without knowing that I have been a blessing to someone who really needs a blessing. We are not called to judge others. We are called to demonstrate to others that God loves them.

And that He gave His only Son to die on a cross so they wouldn't have to. To be forgiven of their sins and have the hope of going to heaven.

WHY DO I THINK THAT THE HOLY SPIRIT IS MISSING?

So, what, or who, is missing in our modern church culture? Clearly, it's the presence of the Holy Spirit. Jesus in me, us. Why do I say that? I think we're trying too hard to please others. And to please ourselves. To fit in. To be accepted. To move up the ladder. Instead, we ought to be trying to please God. **We need to pray every day, "Lord Jesus, may people see you and not me." "May people hear you and not me."** This kind of prayer God, the Holy Spirit, will answer. That would change everything, beginning with an attitude of gratitude.

1 Thessalonians 1:2 (KJV) "In everything give thanks: for this is the will of God in Christ Jesus concerning you."

"I care a lot about you. I want more for you than simply doing well in school or not getting into trouble. I want you to learn that *you are important.* I know you are, but I'm not sure *you* know it." .... **When The Pieces Don't Fit: God Makes The Difference.**....Glaphre Gililand - Zondervan Publishing House

Lord, make me a vessel that brings glory and honor to the Father and bears much fruit in the Lord's kingdom today. One who demonstrates Pure Religion. In the precious name of Jesus. Amen

SOMETHING TO THINK ABOUT:

Does it seem to me that there is less and less interest in church these days?

CHAPTER 3

GENUINE FAITH WORKS

1 John 3:17 (NIV)
If anyone has material possessions and sees his brother in need but has no pity on him, how can the love of God be in him?

18 Dear children, let us not love with words or tongue but with actions and in truth.

WHAT DO YOU MEAN, "FAITH WORKS?"

I write this book for the sake of the poor, the orphans and widows, the homeless, the forgotten, and the abused. I also write it for the masses of people, especially church members, who do not see themselves as participants but observers. After all, that's what we have made them. We cajole people into membership into our churches with the promise that "You're saved. Enjoy your new life." Instead of letting them know that they have "enlisted" in the Lord's army and that every day will involve spiritual warfare where they will have to make serious choices, while at the same time fighting spiritual battles for the souls of others, their neighbors, friends, and co-workers. We assure them that they really don't have to do anything else. Oh, it's O.K., even great, if they would like to participate in some of our church's activities, enroll in a Bible class, or whatever suits them. Meanwhile, they may be thinking, "When do I get to get in the game?" In many churches we don't have a plan or strategy to get them involved in sharing their faith and personally ministering to those in need. **Yes, they need to be trained, educated, and prepared for areas of service. But is this supposed to be their same occupation in the church for years, even decades to come? Many never move past this level. It's too comfortable where they have settled in.**

No wonder it is so rare that we find someone, anyone, in a church today who really exemplifies the examples of the followers of Christ as seen in the Bible. After that great day of Pentecost, when three thousand were baptized into Christ, they even sold their possessions to share with others. Yes, eventually many of them "lost their first love," but were reprimanded by Jesus Himself for doing so. It's pretty hard to get anyone to go visit those in prison, or to the homeless on the streets or in a homeless shelter. I've even heard some say that we shouldn't help them. They've gotten themselves in their messes.

AM I SAVED BY FAITH OR NOT?

In Bible times they did everything by faith. It was by faith that they "believed" in Christ, that He really was the Son of God who had died on the cross that they might be saved. By faith they repented of their sins, confessed Christ as Lord, and were baptized into Him. It was by faith that they accepted the promises of God that they were saved, filled with the Holy Spirit and set apart to do good works that would glorify God. So why would we tell them that they don't have to do anything? **I believe most have accepted Christ because they want to glorify God, the One who made them, and to get involved. And yes, to get to heaven**.

James 2:15-17 (NLT) *Suppose you see a brother or sister who needs food or clothing,*

16 and you say, "Well, good-bye and God bless you; stay warm and eat well," "but then you don't give that person any food or clothing. What good does that do?"

17 So you see, it isn't enough just to have faith. Faith that doesn't show itself by good deeds is no faith at all—it is dead and useless.

DO I HAVE FAITH THAT MOVES MOUNTAINS?

Mama did. She knew God would supply our needs, no matter what. And, because she had faith, she didn't hesitate to ask Brother Dunson for help when he could do what we needed at the time. It took much longer for us to get electricity to our house than for most homes in our area. Simply because, in order to do so it would require putting in the posts and lines from way up the bluff (a small mountain) from the nearest road. Maybe a quarter mile away. Then, taking it across Blackfork creek, as large as many rivers. But one day it happened. But then we would need an electrician to come and wire our house. **Enter Harold Dunson. He had the experience and know-how, and he did wire our old house, which was built many years before. However, before we would finally enjoy electricity right there in our own house, we moved.** This was in 1952. Daddy, who had to find work wherever he could, had gotten a really good job in San Francisco, and decided it was best to move the family, those of us who were left at home (myself, Josie, Grady, Lee, and Grand'Mere) to California. Mama had already moved out there to be with Daddy a few months earlier. We were in San Francisco for only two years when Daddy lost his job as he failed his physical when they were going to transfer him to Barstow, CA. He had advanced sugar diabetes.

The only thing we could do was move back to the "Old Home Place" in Oklahoma. I was very happy about that because I never did like San Francisco during our two-year stay. When we arrived back home, we discovered that our house had been terribly vandalized and trashed. Among other things, all the copper electrical wiring was stripped and gone! The electricity had never even been turned on. Guess what? Mama asked, and brother Harold Dunson came and wired it a second time! **I don't know what kind of a deal our parents had made with him, but I do know he was always willing to do whatever he could for us. Harold demonstrated Pure Religion. Mama demonstrated great faith!**

YOU MEAN THERE'S MORE?

Let me give you one more example of brother Dunson's kindness and generosity. After we came back from San Francisco we had to get everything working again, including our vegetable garden, which was rather large, perhaps 2-3 acres. But now we had no horse with which to plow the garden. So again, Mama asked brother Dunson, our faithful, humble Minister, "would you bring your riding horse, 'Buck,' and plow our garden?" Riding horses aren't meant for plowing. Still, he said "Yes." Keep in mind, we lived several miles from brother Dunson. Not next door. Let me add, the next year brother Dunson's horse, "Buck," was not available to plow our garden. What did we do? **Mama handed me the shovel and said, "I guess you will have do it by yourself this time." I think I said, "The whole thing?"** Mama worked harder than any of us, every day. So, I didn't hesitate to do what she asked. Mama had faith that worked. Taking care of the family. Pure Religion. Yes, there is always more to be done.

Life is a series of daily life challenges. Let's tackle 'em all in His power! Like Mama always said, "Time to get up and get a move on!"

This is probably a good place to talk about another issue. Instead of getting up every day, being excited about opportunities, even ordinary things, helping others, being a blessing, most people are not so inclined. How many of us measure our spirituality by how much we know and have learned about the Bible? Or how many church services we attend? What about all the great discussions we love to have about God and current issues? Do we measure growth by how we see ourselves compared to others? While all these endless exercises are going on in our lives, are we busying ourselves so much that we don't give thought to living out our faith by our actions - outside the comfort zones of our church or group? Do those in need really care how much we know, when what they really want to know is if we care? **<u>Are they even going to listen to us if we won't take the time to get to know them?</u>**

WHY WON'T WE LOOK THEM IN THE EYE?

Not too long ago I attended an adult Sunday School class in between two morning worship services at a church where I was the guest speaker for both services. The Sunday School lesson was from Acts, chapter 3, where Peter and John encountered the lame man as they were about to enter the temple at the time for prayer. The man had been lame from birth, over 40 years ago. Never had walked. When he asked for "alms," money, from Peter and John, it says that they looked "steadfastly" at him. Paraphrasing, they said, "We don't have any money, but what we do have we will give to you. In the Name of Jesus Christ of Nazareth, get up and walk. Taking him by the hand they help him up and he started dancing and praising God." So, in the Sunday School class this story led to two conclusions: one, God doesn't heal in that way today; and, the teacher said, "I just don't look them in the eye," referring to beggars or street people. "If you do, they'll just ask you for something." **I kept waiting for the teacher to say something positive about this incredible event that had happened in Acts three. It never came**.

When I told Sally, my wife, I said that I didn't speak up at the time. I didn't want to create a scene, being the guest speaker that day, with another service yet to go. She said, "you should have spoken up. If I had been there, I would have said something!" **I knew she was right. The thought came to me while I was sitting there listening to the teacher, "Then, how are they going to know that God loves them?"** I think a lot of church members, some who are even faithful Christians, think, "That's not my problem. They will have to learn that from somebody else. I don't want to be taken advantage of. Anyway, I'm saved and on my way to heaven. What difference will it make whether I do or don't tell that God loves them?"

ARE THERE ANY "GOOD SAMARITANS" LEFT IN THE WORLD?

I've often thought about all the people in need. Certainly, if I don't have the gift of healing, how could I have healed the lame man? No, but I can help. This is exactly what the Samaritan (Luke 10:30-37), a foreigner, did when he stopped to help someone who had been beaten, robbed, and left for dead. He could not heal him, but he did help him. Bandaged his wounds. Took him to a hotel. Paid for his expenses. Don't you know that the man he did all these things for was wondering, "Who is this? I never expected to be treated so kindly." Friend, this is Jesus' love in action. This is Pure Religion! If you or I can't heal, we can help. Jesus said, "Love your neighbor

26

as yourself." Your neighbor is anyone in need. **Can we pray every day that God would use us to be a special blessing to someone?**

HOW DO YOU SEE IT?

I don't have an agenda here. I'm not just trying to get you to agree with me and see things my way. I'm still learning and, I hope, growing. I invite you to do the same. Every day it seems I learn something new - even from Scriptures I have known since my childhood. Every day I ask the Holy Spirit to be pro-active in my life, operating in everything I say and do, see and hear. I look for signs of the Lord's Presence everywhere: In relationships; activities. As I write this, I am looking forward to going to a local men's jail to conduct evening worship services. **I'm excited!**

Why? Because it's Jesus I am going to see. Locked up! And I will be His voice. His hands and feet to these men. I am going in His name. We will have a great time. It doesn't get any better than this!

James 2:8 (NLT*) Yes indeed, it is good when you truly obey our Lord's royal command found in the Scriptures: "Love your neighbor as yourself."*

"Our Lord asks us to love our neighbors as we love ourselves. This is the second great command. In heaven and on earth, love is the royal law." **Love Is Supreme...Andrew Murray**...Multnomah Books

Dear Lord, may my desire today be to love everyone with the same love with which You have loved me. May it be Pure Religion in Your eyes, Lord. In Jesus' Name

SOMETHING TO THINK ABOUT:

Do you feel that your faith is active enough?

CHAPTER 4

WHAT DO YOU DO WHEN YOU'VE NEVER DONE IT BEFORE?

Luke 4:18 (NKJV)
"The Spirit of the LORD is upon Me, Because He has anointed Me To preach the gospel to the poor; He has sent Me to heal the brokenhearted, To proclaim liberty to the captives And recovery of sight to the blind, To set at liberty those who are oppressed."

WAS IT TIME TO "PUT UP" OR, "SHUT UP?"

Sally and I both were raised in very strong, Christian families. And yet, we were facing something neither of us had actually had much experience doing - going into the deep, inner city to minister, and establishing a church for the homeless, the poor, and for convicts - ex-convicts and future convicts. When we met in 1987, we soon realized that we both had an overwhelming desire to do something more meaningful for God than we had ever done before. We were both in mid-life at this time. We believed God was bringing us together in marriage, and to glorify Him through what we would call, "Caring Ministries". While we didn't incorporate that title, what we did soon begin would be to establish Memphis Inner City Outreach. **We believed God, the Holy Spirit, was leading us to minister specifically to the poorest and most needy in inner city Memphis.**

It would also be the beginning of a prison ministry at 201 Poplar, the Shelby County Jail. (I have recently returned there to conduct worship services several times a month on Wednesday evenings. Such a special time for me - again.) Soon, we began going downtown on weekends taking clothing, refreshments, and shelter vouchers to people living on the streets. We began our street ministry the first two weekends in late December 1988. The temperature was five below zero, without the wind-chill! Out of an old van we shared hot coffee & chocolate, sandwiches, tube socks, gloves, skullcaps, and free "shelter vouchers", which would allow them to stay overnight at either the Memphis Union Mission, the Salvation Army, or at Calvary Rescue Mission. Clearly, it was a big hit! Among the volunteers who often went with us on Saturdays were Sally's daughter, Ellen - and her two-year-old son, Justin, giving out sandwiches to the homeless! They fell in love with him and looked forward to seeing him whenever he would come. We very much enjoyed getting to know a lot of the street people personally, even learning their street names and "nicknames." **<u>Sadly, we soon became aware that the longer they were on the street, the harder it was for them to get off the streets.</u>** We endeavored to help many of them to do just that. Sally and I were both still working full-time during the week, Sally as a Court Reporter, myself as a full-time Evangelist. We couldn't wait for the next Saturday when we would again go share with the homeless, and Wednesday nights at the Jail.

WERE WE DOING THIS FOR THE RIGHT REASON?

A very good friend of mine, Joanie Grimm, an extremely talented musician and national children's worker, came to share with us during the first year of our Memphis Inner City Church. She saw our excitement as things were really going great. Then, she said something we didn't expect: **"Why are you doing this? If it's for them, when it's all said and done, most of them won't care; If it's for yourselves, you will soon grow very tired of it; It must be for God, and God alone."** We felt like we could say, truthfully, "It's for God, and God alone."

We had been praying fervently for at least a year about doing this. We knew that God was leading us in this direction. Our goal was to use this street ministry to lay the foundation for something much more significant, namely, establishing a church for inner city people, within a year. These were those who were not likely to be going to any established church, except maybe for a meal or clothing handout. This church would be later described by one of its members as, "The Church where anyone could go!" I loved it! Would this even work, having a church specifically targeting the homeless and the poor, as well as drug addicts, alcoholics, prostitutes? One of our more upstanding, "inner city" members pulled me aside one day and said, **"You may not know it, but there are a lot of people coming to your church here with serious problems: drug addicts, etc......."** **I said, "Yes, that's why we're here!"** A lot of people came for the first time out of curiosity, seeing changed lives of people whom they knew coming to Christ, and now living totally different, new lives.

WAS THIS JUST ANOTHER "STREET" MINISTRY?

It wasn't just a street ministry for very long. We soon began to expand, and Sally and I did everything as a team. Some things I would do by myself, such as going to the Memphis Mental Health facilities to sing and share with them; visiting and ministering at several homeless shelters; delivering "Meals On Wheels." The two things we primarily did together were making (what seemed like) hundreds of sandwiches every weekend on our small kitchen table to take downtown on Saturdays to the homeless. We went wherever we could find them, whether just one, or in groups. We began to take other things as well, such as hygiene kits. We soon began weekly services at the Shelby County Jail at 201 Poplar on Wednesday nights. This was, and still is, the largest County Jail in the State of Tennessee, with several thousand inmates. This would become one of the most beneficial and productive activities we would do, as it put us in contact with so many who would need ministering to, during incarceration and upon their release, after incarceration. **After all, how many churches want known, "Ex-convicts" sitting in their church services?** Hundreds came to Christ and were baptized in a baptistry, donated by ARM, American Rehabilitation Ministries, Joplin, MO, Joe Garman, Director, at the Shelby County Jail over the next several years. Now, 30 years later, that baptistry, located in the chapel, is still being used on a regular basis. Perhaps thousands have been "buried with Christ" in that baptistry. We were excited and being so blessed by these activities that we invited everyone we could think of to go with us. One week we surprised everyone by bringing a summer teen choir that I was directing for Mid-South Christian College that we called, "I Witness," to present a special concert for the inmates. The packed chapel of inmates loved it! Even the choir members, high schoolers from through the mid-south churches, said, "This was our favorite place to sing for the whole tour"! Almost all of our friends who did go to the jail with us had the same reaction, "This is great!"

HOW WOULD WE KNOW THAT THIS WAS GOD'S PLAN - NOT JUST OURS?

Once we announced the beginning of this inner-city ministry, the Holy Spirit began to open doors that literally amazed us. Everything

31

we would need began to fall into place, including volunteers and donations. Tim Anderson, Youth Minister at Crestview Christian Church, brought a team to help us with an outdoor Vacation Bible School for kids living in the Lauderdale Courts Public Housing Project, in the summer of 1990, in the exact neighborhood where the new church would soon be located. A wonderful family from First Christian Church, Brookport, IL, spent an entire weekend helping us clean up trash and broken glass in the neighborhood, and to prepare a warehouse, in just one day, Saturday, before our first Sunday services, where we would meet for

the next seven years. I sang on a local gospel music T. V. program that Steve and Christy Bradford had at the time, announcing our plans to begin the inner-city ministry. As a result, that night I got a call from a prominent citizen, a Christian, who worked with the Memphis Police Department Youth Boxing Program, located in Lauderdale Courts. He said, **"Whatever you need for your ministry, including a place to meet, just let me know. I will help you!"** At our Wednesday night Shelby County Jail service, another Christian volunteer who was in attendance, said, "Let me know where you are going to meet next Sunday. My wife and I will be there." He was a former college basketball player, now living and working in Memphis. He and his wife would be a part of the church as members and teachers for years to come. The need for just the right building to begin the church had now become an urgent need. Then, by the Holy Spirit's leading, with only three days left before opening Sunday, we agreed with a local businessman to rent a warehouse, in a strategic location. **I signed the contract on Saturday night, just before our first Sunday service. It was a perfect first building for the new Memphis Inner City Church and Outreach Ministries.** The warehouse served us well for those seven years until we could buy property and start building new facilities, located just half block away. When God calls and sends, He provides!

WHY WERE SO MANY OTHERS NOW WANTING TO GET INVOLVED?

There are just too many stories to get into about how God provided in unexpected ways for every activity and every need. The Holy Spirit led us step by step in this incredible new venture. Our primary motive was to follow wherever God would lead. Over the next few years, we would see church after church getting involved with us. There were very dynamic individuals and families that the Spirit led to us to become a vital part of this ministry, not only from the greater Memphis area churches, but also from the downtown area. **Volunteers even came from employees at Juvenile Court as well as churches in Germantown, Collierville, and Bartlett, to tutor the scores of kids coming to the new church.** We gained Sunday School teachers, Clothes Closet volunteers, and workers for our men's ministry activities. Groups from churches out of state came to bring groups of volunteers to do whatever was needed. Our summer youth programs, such as Vacation Bible School, featured very talented groups of youth and adults who would literally take over to do, and provide, whatever was needed for the hundreds who were becoming a part of our church and outreach ministries. Truckloads of clothing for our Clothes Closet came from other states. One day while I was sorting through a load of clothes we had just received, a $20 bill fell out of the pocket of a pair of jeans. **As I kept looking, I discovered a total of $640 in that one pair of jeans. I could just imagine a teenager, somewhere, asking, "Mom, have you seen my jeans"? "Well, yes, I donated them to that new mission in**

Memphis!" We became a magnet for so many just wanting to participate with us and serve others. This became for them an opportunity to participate in "Pure Religion".

It's something powerfully spiritual when the Holy Spirit touches your heart with something radically different from anything you have ever done before. When we say "Yes" to the Spirit's leading, all the resources of heaven are at our disposal. So much of what many of us do with our time, talents, and resources is just for our own agenda, which allows for only rare occurrences of practicing "Pure Religion." Even then, we know what a tremendous blessing awaits anyone who gets involved and shares with others, especially those most in need, the unconditional love of Jesus.

JUST HOW LONG DO YOU THINK YOU WILL BE HERE?

As we continued to establish this new church, with outreach ministries, some of our church members and visitors, started to ask, "How long do you plan to be here? We've seen a lot of people like you come and go!" They would add, "A lot of groups or individuals just use us for publicity, or to please themselves, that they really care - when they don't, because none of them stay. Two years at the most." We knew that it was only by the grace of God that we were there in the first place. It would also be the grace of God by which we would stay - as long as He determined we would. I remember, after we had been there over ten years, through many different programs and activities, two new building programs, hundreds of members and workers, one of the older men stood to speak before the congregation in the Sunday morning service. **He turned to me, standing behind him on the stage, and said, "I've seen a lot of men come and go. But you're still standing!" (I felt like a boxing champion!)** That meant more to him, and to me, than you could ever

34

know. This man had been at our very first Sunday morning service in September 1990. When he moved out of the projects to a modest home a few streets away, he would drive his old, forty-foot, Cadillac to church, many times bringing others with him. When he died of old age, I was honored to conduct his funeral. I, along with all of his family, celebrated a very humble man who loved the Lord very much. How can you not have pride in seeing what the Lord had done through this one man. He was not the only one who noticed that we had not soon given up. Other members told us the same thing as he did about stay and not giving up. **See what we miss when we neglect, or ignore, the Holy Spirit's leading to practice "Pure Religion?"**

I WAS NO LONGER SATISFIED!

In the early and mid 1980s, in the years leading up the start of this inner-city ministry, I was personally, desperately seeking the Lord. In all, I traveled 20 years in evangelism before we began Memphis Inner City Outreach in 1989. I was really drained and running on empty, spiritually and mentally. I was no longer satisfied (happy and contented) to just keep doing what I had been doing for so long. **I knew that the Holy Spirit was speaking very loudly to my heart, "There's more! Much more!"** For me the serious search for what was the Lord's will take serval years. I sought the most personal relationship I could ever possibly have with the Lord. In my early morning devotions. In my ministering through music and preaching. And, in my attitude. It took years for me to become so self-centered and self-righteous. **Now, I needed to allow God to dismantle all of self in me. Once in Memphis and seeing the beginning of our new mission to the inner city, I began praying daily for compassion for the homeless and the poor of Memphis**. We were about to commit to ministering primarily to the African American population. And, to the poorest of those. In the city where Dr. Martin Luther King, Jr. was assassinated, we would soon make our church home with this community. It would have to be genuine, "Pure Religion."

"In our society, we tend to swear unyielding allegiance to a rigid position, confusing that action with finding an authentic connection to a life-giving Spirit. We miss the gospel of Christ: the good news that, although the Holy and all-powerful God knows we are dust, He still stoops to breathe into us the breath of life - to bring our wounds the balm of acceptance and love." .... Rich Mullins testimony - **The Ragamuffin Gospel, Brennan Manning.**....Multnomah Press

Proverbs 19:17 *"He who is kind to the poor lends to the LORD, and he will reward him for what he has done."*

Heavenly Father may Your Holy Spirit anoint and guide me today to be kind to the poor, and by Your Holy Spirit, love as Jesus loves. In His Name. Amen

SOMETHING TO THINK ABOUT:

Have you ever been asked to do something that seemed a little too radical for you?

CHAPTER 5

WOULD WE BE THE "MATTHEW 25" CHURCH?

Matthew 25:35-36 (NIV)
"For I was hungry, and you gave me something to eat, I was thirsty and you gave me something to drink, I was a stranger and you invited me in, 36 I needed clothes and you clothed me, I was sick and you looked after me, I was in prison and you came to visit me."

COULD THIS BE THE REAL MEANING OF "PURE RELIGION?"

I believe the definition of "pure" is clear; spotless; unadulterated. And I believe it also alludes to being genuine. Authentic. How many times have you heard someone say they just want to be "real?" But then we go on like we have always been, thinking that we have always been "real." It's the other people that need to understand what "pure" really means.

As to Matthew, chapter 25, I believe we see clearly an expanded definition of "Pure Religion," and what was important to Jesus. How many of us actually make these our priorities as well? Not many. Never mind that Jesus is referring to what will matter - on Judgement Day! So, <u>am I</u> going to pay more attention to the things he mentions in Matthew 25: hunger; thirst; strangers; no clothes; sickness; or in prison, <u>only if</u> that's what it takes to get into heaven? Is it possible that He is really talking about actually wanting to help others? Loving so much, like He does, that we can't resist helping others? **<u>Even if we "fake it," we still have to answer to God for what's in our hearts.</u>** Have we prayed for compassion? Have we prayed for humility? Have we prayed that He would open our eyes to see those around us, and for opportunities to be a blessing to someone every day? We are all in the same boat. Just when I think I have seen a "super" Christian, I find out that everyone has had to come by the same route of humility and surrender of self before they can be truly used of God. **<u>"Pure Religion" only happens in us when we allow or ask the Lord for it.</u>** The Holy Spirit then puts the love of Jesus in us. That's when we realize that we have "died" and it's no longer me, but Him. Simply put, Jesus is love. I don't have to "fake it" anymore!

DO WE HAVE ANY CURRENT EXAMPLES OF PURE RELIGION?

The Memphis Inner City Church and Outreach Ministries would not have been possible, would not have survived, without certain key people. I can't begin to include all who fit in that category here, but certain ones stand out. **<u>Sally, my wife, is one of those at the very top. She was a great prayer-warrior, every step of the way, trusting God for all that we would need. And stepping out in faith to do whatever was needed</u>**. Among other things she: played the piano for worship services; organized the teen and adult choirs, both of whom we took on tours throughout the mid-south churches to raise funds for the new building program; taught every level of youth Sunday School classes; sometimes refereed teenagers who were going at each other; plus, being a tremendous encouragement to me and an advocate for this mission. She did all of this while still working full-time as a Court Reporter. She retired after a 50-year career.

I earlier mentioned Sally's daughter, Ellen, a nurse at the Regional Medical Center, as one of the volunteers who got involved early on, even before the church was established. Then, along with her husband Mark, they brought their family every Sunday for the first five years, even though they lived quite a way out from the church. Ellen taught Sunday School, helped with special events, raised funds, recruited more volunteers, and truly went the extra mile in whatever needed to be done.

Then, we were also blessed when Sally's parents, Vernon and Helen Watkins, announced that they would also be making the Inner-City Church their home church. They not only lived out in Millington, almost an hour's drive one way, but Helen would be coming in a wheelchair. The kids loved pushing Helen's wheelchair to the classroom where she taught a Sunday School class. Vernon made wonderful contributions with his carpentry skills, building the stage in our first new building, and building cabinets and storage units for our food pantry. Vernon, a Bible College graduate, was also a great Bible teacher. They came for the first seven years when they said, **"We're not going to be able to continue coming down to the church because of health reasons." They were both in their 80s. They filled such a need. "Pure Religion."**

WERE LIVES REALLY BEING CHANGED?

Let me introduce you to a couple of other outstanding people who became a part of Memphis Inner City Church. Ellen, (not Sally's daughter) at first said, "I don't want to hear about your church! Please, quit trying to get me to come!" She lived across the street from our (warehouse) church in an eight-story high rise apartment building, Barry Homes. One of our Associate Ministers was talking to Ellen one day at the high rise, telling her about the great things God was doing in this new church, when she lashed out at him, cursing, "I don't want to hear it!" Ray, our associate, could be very convincing. But not this time. Eventually, however, Ellen kept seeing people she knew who were radically changed for the better as a result of attending the church and accepting Christ. Her curiosity finally got the better of her and she came for the first time when we dedicated our first new building, Mother's Day, 1997. She came again the next week. And the next. Within a couple of months, Ellen surrendered her life to Christ. When we baptized her, she stood up in the baptistry, soaking wet, looked around at the audience and said, **"You all know me. You know if God can save me, He can save anybody!"** Ellen had a very difficult life. At age eight, she watched in horror as her stepdad murdered her mom in their home. Everything went downhill from there. She became hardened against God and against men. She became very tough, living on the streets and adopting a lifestyle that she would refer to as her "gaylationships." We later learned that she had never worn a skirt or dress, until Sally helped her to start dressing like a woman. When I first met her, I honestly didn't know if she was a male or female, based on the way she dressed and wore her hair. She and I would later have some good laughs about that. She thought it was hilarious! When Ellen accepted Christ, she also threw out her worldly music and declared, "I've joined the choir". When she went on tour with us, she would publicly testify that God had saved her from her "gaylationship" lifestyle and given her a whole new life. She became

40

a "greeter" at the church with the biggest smile anyone would see at our church. **One night, after choir rehearsal, during prayer time, she prayed, softly, "God, I would die for this church."** I was blown away. Because I knew she meant it.

MEET "IRVIN."

The second person I want to tell you about was a homeless man named "Irvin." Every Sunday I would go down to the church about an hour early to get things ready for another day of services, make coffee, arrange the clothes closet, set up the sound system, and anything else that needed to be done. I began to notice that in the parking lot there were small piles of trash, and liquor bottles, that had been neatly arranged for picking up to clear the area before people would be arriving. That's when I first met Irvin. He was very shy. He would say very few words. He wouldn't even come inside when services began. I believe the Lord was preparing him, and us, for many blessings to come. He had once been a successful salesman, traveling cross country, making big money. But, as he told me, "I drank like a fish!" Eventually he did begin to come inside. But it would be months, maybe a couple of years, before he gained the confidence, and trust in us, to actually get up front and talk about his faith in Christ. **He would introduce himself simply as, "Irvin." He would tell the young people, "Get your education. Stay in school. Give your life to Jesus."** Irvin, because he had become so loved and trusted by everyone, was eventually given a whole set of keys to the building. We made room for him to live there. One day Irvin said to me, "It looks like I will be going back to Denver where I used to live. I have received enough money to take the Amtrak train back home." We were both very happy and very sad as we took him to the train station. We were losing a very loving and trusted friend that we had now known for many years. Once back in Denver, he faithfully sent back Christmas and birthday cards to several of us for years, calling us his "friends." Thank you, Lord, for people like Irvin. We were blessed.

ONE OF OUR MEMBERS ASKED, "WOULD IT BE MURDER?"

Lavinnia J., one of our faithful, senior members living in Barry Homes High Rise across the street, showed up at our Thursday afternoon Bible Study with a very interesting situation. **"I know the Bible says, 'Do not kill.' Does that include cock roaches?"** she asked. She was serious. She was one of the sweetest people you would ever meet. So, why not be sure that God wasn't including cock roaches in His command not to kill? I assured her that God didn't mean don't kill bugs, of any kind. He even told Peter to, "Rise, kill and eat!" John the Baptist even ate locusts, dipped in honey. Why tell this story? We came to know so many special people through our inner-city ministry, most of whom lived very simple lives. They wanted the Lord to be Lord in every area of their lives, even pesky cock roaches!

IS IT TOO DIFFICULT TO UNDERSTAND?

It's not that hard to see what Jesus would do if He were in the same situations I am describing here. I confess that, on my own, I would probably not be interested in going out of my way to reach out to those we sometimes call "losers." But, as I read it, Jesus says that He is now the One who is doing these things. We are merely His instruments. After washing the disciples feet, he said in **John 13:15, (KJV)** *"For I have given you an example, that you should do as I have done to you."* He also tells us in **Ephesians 5:1-2, (NIV)** *"Be* *imitators of God, therefore, as dearly loved children, 2 and live a life of love, just as Christ loved us and gave himself up for us as a fragrant offering and sacrifice to God.*" And, what about this? **John 15:5, (NKJV)** *"I am the vine, you are the branches. He who abides in Me, and I in him, bears much fruit; for without Me you can do nothing."*

We can pretend that we do not know or understand what our Lord is trying to get us to do. I truly believe that the Holy Spirit is constantly pointing us toward practicing "Pure Religion." How? By the people and circumstances, we see around us every day, particularly, the people we know Jesus would never ignore. I once heard a prominent minister and great preacher say, "Are we building His kingdom, or our own little "kingdoms?" Are we about "Our Father's business," our own denominational agendas? Just ask people in your church, **"Are we really doing what the Lord wants? Or, just what we want?"**

WOULD YOU LIKE TO HEAR THE "REST OF THE STORY?"

After almost 20 years on location, the Memphis Inner City Church closed its doors. We had seen God do so many tremendous things in those years. So many lives were changed by the power of the gospel of Christ. The love of Christ was visibly seen in the lives of His people as a result of the Inner-City Church, and Outreach Ministries. However, we were in a very transient part of town: Public Housing; homelessness; poverty. Most of our church members came from Lauderdale Courts Public Housing Project, located between Exchange Avenue, Third Street, and Danny Thomas Blvd, near St Jude Hospital. At that time over 2,000 people lived in that small area. After we built our first new building in 1997, we met with the City of Memphis Development Director as to whether or not to build a second building, a gymnasium auditorium. They were making plans to either tear down Lauderdale Courts or to renovate into upscale housing. So, I asked, "If we build this addition to our building, would the people still be living here?" "Of course," they said. So we built again in 2001, only to realize that only about five percent of the people living in Lauderdale Courts would be returning.

The new residents moving in across the street were very upscale business types. Rent was very high, ranging from a low of $500 a month to $1500 a month. Not exactly suited for the poor. Now, there was even a fence around the whole property, making it impossible to enter the grounds without going to their office for permission. That included distributing any church newsletters or literature, which I had done since the beginning of the church in 1990. Even though we were an outreach church, we made every effort to get these new families into our congregation. They weren't that excited to come and sit with the homeless and ex-convicts attending our church. We began to send several vans, even an old school bus, into housing projects out of our immediate area in order to bring new people who could be a part of the church. By now, there were several very successful "Inner City Churches," whereas we were the only one when we started. Volunteers and funds coming from outlying areas of Memphis was now mostly gone. Even though in our last couple of years we baptized about 100 new believers into Christ, we no longer had the staff and funds necessary to continue. For several years I had become more of an administrator and fund-raiser than a Minister / Pastor, due to the increased pressures facing us, including building payments. Our Board of Directors advised that we close the church and thank God for the many victories over the years. This was not an easy decision. Those left in the church would not understand what we did about our situation. God had been so good, so faithful, to bless us with the greatest blessings in our lives. **It was, at the same time, also the most traumatic experience in our lives. Sally said it best. "It was like losing a child."**

NOW, WHAT WERE WE GOING TO DO?

It would have been easy to just move on to something, out of the inner city. Instead, God began to open doors for me to resume what we had done during the first year, before the church began. Doors opened at Juvenile Court, Mark Luttrell Prison, Juvenile Court, Memphis Union Mission, and the CCA Men's Prison in Whiteville, TN. Since 2007, ministering in these facilities, we have seen literally hundreds come to Christ and being baptized into Him. Yes, praise the Lord even for doors closing, as He opens new doors we would never see otherwise. We choose to go on to wherever He wants us, to see opportunities to practice "Pure Religion."

Job 42:2 (NIV) *"I know that you can do all things; no plan of yours can be thwarted."*

Lord, thank You for Your power to do all things according to Your will. I ask You to give me the faith to accept Your control over every aspect of my life! In Jesus' Name. Amen

SOMETHING TO THINK ABOUT:

How would you describe a church, "Where anyone can go?

CHAPTER 6

ISN'T "PURE RELIGION" REALLY "PERFECT LOVE?"

1 John 2:10 (MSG)
"It's the person who loves brother and sister who dwells in God's light and doesn't block the light from others."

1 John 4:7 (AV)
"Beloved, let us love one another: for love is of God; and everyone that loveth is born of God, and knoweth God.

8 He that loveth not knoweth not God; for God is love."

1 John 3:23-24 (NIV)
"And this is his command: to believe in the name of his Son, Jesus Christ, and to love one another as he commanded us.

24 Those who obey his commands live in him, and he in them. And this is how we know that he lives in us: We know it by the Spirit, he gave us."

SO, IS IT EVEN POSSIBLE TO LOVE LIKE JESUS LOVES?

Pray! Pray! Pray! Practice! Practice! Practice! Is it not virtually impossible to love our enemies? Or, to love someone who has hurt us terribly? On our own, yes! One of the things that has helped me in recent years is to pray every morning, "Lord, you are Lord of my life, King of my heart. Help me to see everyone today as You see them, and to respond accordingly." Some of my favorite Bible verses (below) remind me that it's no longer me, but Jesus, living in me. It's the only way I can ever hope to obey His commands (as described in the above verses) to love difficult people. And this is the attitude and mind-set I must take with me every day. The Holy Spirit will gladly honor my request to be Jesus to others. If I preach love and practice love, by His grace, I will have love. **Essentially, I love God as much as I love the ones, I love the least.**

Galatians 2:20 (NKJV) *"I have been crucified with Christ; it is no longer I who live, but Christ lives in me; and the life which I now live in the flesh I live by faith in the Son of God, who loved me and gave Himself for me."*

Philippians 4:13 (NKJV) *"I can do all things through Christ who strengthens me."*

Colossians 3:3 (NKJV) *"For you died, and your life is hidden with Christ in God."*

DOES GOD STILL LOVE ME, EVEN AFTER KNOWING EVERYTHING ABOUT ME?

I often go to talk to juveniles who are in trouble. Some in very deep trouble. One day I received a call from one of the supervisors at Juvenile Court asking, "When you come down the next time, would you mind talking to a young man who was just arrested and was brought here and charged with murdering a younger sibling? (He had been put in isolation, as he was a danger to others) I can't get him to talk to me. He won't even look at me." We were taken to a private room, and when I sat at a table across from him, he had his head down, not looking at me. After I introduced myself, I said, "God knows everything about you - and still loves you." He then raised his head and looked straight at me as I continued talking. **I really don't remember much of what I said in the next 12-15 minutes, but he never took his eyes off me.** I prayed for him and shook his hand before leaving. In a year or so he was transferred to Jail East to be with other teens who are being tried as adults.

He was faithful to be in every Bible Study and worship service that I, and others, conducted. He accepted Christ as his Lord and Savior and was baptized into Christ.

None of us can judge him, even if we have doubts about his motive or sincerity. I can say that I detected a definite change in his personality. He was no longer angry nor confused. He was no longer a threat, but calm. Yes, he will have to account for his actions through the court system with perhaps a very stiff sentence. **He is not the first teen I have seen come into the system, having committed a terrible crime, who was visibly changed after being exposed to the love of God and surrendering to Christ. And, going on to serving "hard time."**

DOES GOD EVER SAY "NO?"

No. Not when anyone calls on Him from the heart. Just think of all the prominent characters whose stories we read in the Bible who once were totally alienated from God that it would take a miracle to win them over to Him. Well, God is still performing the greatest miracles of all, lives changed by the love of Christ. How does God do it? Through you and me. But not if we are not willing to be used.

You might say, "That's not really my thing, to go to prisons, to the homeless, or to a foreign country." That's not the point. Aren't we called to be Jesus, wherever we are? Isn't it really a matter of the heart? And mind? Doesn't it come down to asking the Lord, "What do you want to do through me"? And then giving Him total permission to use us? **People know whether you love them with the love of Christ, or not. It's who we are meant to be.**

"JENNY, WHY DON'T YOU LOVE ME?"

Ever seen the movie, "Forest Gump?" Most people in the U. S. have. Do you remember when Forest put his hands on his hips and, out of frustration, asked the love of his life, "Jenny, I know what love is. Why don't you love me?" He had loved Jenny since they were kids, but she saw him as just a friend. And although he did everything for her, she was not "in love" with him. **Do you think maybe God is asking us, "Why don't you love me?"**

Love is demonstrating kindness. Since we grew up very poor, I seem to be drawn to the poor, or neglected. I like to go just a little bit out of my way to be kind to them. One example: Many years ago, I was leading a revival meeting in Ohio. We were seeing God do great things. Great spirit. Great crowds and fellowship. I noticed, among those coming in the lobby, two teen-age sisters. They were somewhat overweight, but very friendly. I took a little time to talk to them, to get to know them. After a night or two, they asked to talk to me. **"Are you for real, being so friendly to us? Or, is it what you feel you have to do?"** I didn't often get a question like that. I assured them that I was not being phoney. I don't remember what happened to them, as there were hundreds coming to the revival. But I have never forgotten this incident. It is so important that we always treat people with love and kindness, even if we don't suspect they might have a problem with insecurity. What would Jesus do? Just what he did to the rich young ruler in the gospel of Mark, chapter 10. It says,

"Jesus, beholding him, loved him," That's something we all can do!

SO, WHY AREN'T MORE OF US MORE LIKE JESUS?

My opinion is that we are the ones who might be insecure. Even though in Christ we are saved, redeemed, restored, and filled with the Holy Spirit, we are still dealing with our own self-image, which we don't like. If I don't like me, you won't like me either. I recently read where a Christian teacher challenged the audience to look at someone and say, "God really, really loves me!" We would normally say, "God loves you"! I can see the purpose in changing the question. If I know that God really, really loves me, you can be pretty sure that I will love you too! And you can be sure that if God loves me, He loves you also. I will sometimes counsel teens in Juvenile Detention by saying, "If you don't feel loved, or have any value, you can be dangerous. Why? Because if you don't think anyone really cares about you, even God, what does it matter what you do?" **There are way too many kids being brought into the world today who are unloved, neglected, abandoned, abused, and told repeatedly, "You're no good! You will never amount to anything! You're nothing but trouble!"** So, many of them set out to fulfill that image, even hating themselves. I have found that when I start telling them, "I believe you are created in the image of God, and that he has a special purpose and plan for you," there is an immediate change in their expressions. Perhaps they have never had anyone tell them that God loves them, no matter what, and that He gave His Son, Jesus to die on a cross, in their place, to forgive them of their sins.

Jesus spent his entire life on earth to not only save us, but to also show us how to love and connect with others. You and I know how much it means to people to know that they are loved, and chosen by their Creator to be like Jesus, to be "real." Max Lucado put it well when he writes, ***"In essence Christianity is nothing more, nothing less, than a desire and an effort to see Jesus. That's all it is. We're trying to catch a glimpse of a man - not a doctrine. We're trying to see a man who called himself the Son of God."*** - **Walking With The Savior** - Tyndale. It has always been our Father's will, and plan for us, to become more and more like Jesus. The Bible says in **1 John 3:2-3 (NKJV)** *"Beloved, now we are children of God; and it has not yet been revealed what we shall be, but we know that when He is revealed, we shall be like Him, for we shall see Him as He is."*

HAS ANYONE EVER SAID, "I SEE JESUS IN YOU?"

Perhaps they may have said it differently, but implied it just the same. It's very humbling. Why would someone say that to you? If they meant it, it will be because they observed you being like Jesus. I think the best description of this can be found in Philippians, chapter two. Bottom line, it comes down to humility. **When we act selfishly, or arrogantly, we are the opposite of who Jesus was.** I've even known, and worked with, ministers who threatened bodily harm to someone if they didn't act a certain way. I don't think Jesus ever threatened anyone in that way. What He did do was to promise that those who threatened or cursed Him would see the judgment of God come upon them. Because He came to serve and not to be served, He demonstrated the importance of self-denial. On the other hand, we want to let it be known that we can handle anything, on our own. **Thank God for Jesus!**

Philippians 2:5-11 (NKJV) *"Let this mind be in you which was also in Christ Jesus,*

6 who, being in the form of God, did not consider it robbery to be equal with God,

7 but made Himself of no reputation, taking the form of a bondservant, and coming in the likeness of men.

8 And being found in appearance as a man, He humbled Himself and became obedient to the point of death, even the death of the cross.

9 Therefore God also has highly exalted Him and given Him the name, which is above every name,

10 that at the name of Jesus every knee should bow, of those in heaven, and of those on earth, and of those under the earth,

11 and that every tongue should confess that Jesus Christ is Lord, to the glory of God the Father."

Galatians 6:14 (KJV) *"But God forbid that I should glory, save in the cross of our Lord Jesus Christ, by whom the world is crucified unto me, and I unto the world."*

WHAT CAN WE TAKE AWAY FROM THIS CHAPTER?

I think that we are it, His vessels. Jesus isn't coming back to live in the flesh. But what He has done is to promise, "I will be with you." *"I will never leave you nor forsake you."*

Matthew 28:20 (NIV) *"And surely I am with you always, to the very end of the age."*

Hebrews 13:5 (NKJV) *"For He Himself has said, "I will never leave you nor forsake you."*

John 14:18 (NIV) *"I will not leave you as orphans; I will come to you."*

John 14:16 -17 (NLT) *"And I will ask the Father, and he will give you another Counselor, who will never leave you.*

17 He is the Holy Spirit, who leads into all truth."

He is more here now than He was back then. The sooner we learn to truly love one another - and show it, the sooner we will be effectively "turning the world upside down" for Him. I think we have a way to go. **We are, perhaps, too much about our programs and preferences than we are about loving others or seeking the lost.**

Do we have any idea how much it means to someone to know that you truly care for them? That you're not just faking it? We're not just talking about those close to us. What about people in so many third world countries who have needs we cannot even imagine? I have been so blessed to visit and share Jesus in many countries. I cannot describe how much their thanks and gratitude affect my life. I want to be "real," and be Jesus to them.

Isaiah 58:6-8 (NKJV) *"Is this not the fast that I have chosen: To loose the bonds of wickedness, To undo the heavy burdens, To let the oppressed go free, And that you break every yoke?*

7 Is it not to share your bread with the hungry, And that you bring to your house the poor who are cast out; When you see the naked, that you cover him, And not hide yourself from your own flesh?

8 Then your light shall break forth like the morning, Your healing shall spring forth speedily, And your righteousness shall go before you; The glory of the LORD shall be your rear guard."

Lord Jesus, may I let my light shine, daily, that others may see my good deeds, and glorify our Father in heaven. In your name. Amen

SOMETHING TO THINK ABOUT:

How do I know that I am truly loved, or, that I truly love someone?

CHAPTER 7

"AM I REALLY PREPARED FOR THIS?"

Matthew 19:14 (NKJV*)***
But Jesus said, "Let the little children come to Me, and do not forbid them; for of such is the kingdom of heaven."

15 And He laid His hands on them and departed from there.

2 Timothy 3:14-15 (NKJV)
"But as for you, continue in what you have learned and have become convinced of, because you know those from whom you learned it,

15 and how from infancy you have known the holy Scriptures, which are able to make you wise for salvation through faith in Christ Jesus."

Matthew 5:14-16
"You are the light of the world. A city on a hill cannot be hidden.

15 Neither do people light a lamp and put it under a bowl. Instead, they put it on its stand, and it gives light to everyone in the house.

16 In the same way, let your light shine before men, that they may see your good deeds and praise your Father in heaven."

DID GOD HAVE MY FUTURE PLANNED IN ADVANCE?

I'll be honest, I was a little more than just insecure as a kid. I was intimated at the idea that I, the youngest in the family, would ever do anything in life that would really matter. By the time I finished High School and headed for Ozark Bible College, I already had two brothers there, Lee and Grady, and one, Cecil, who had already graduated. My sister, Josie enrolled at the same time that I did. Even worse, Cecil had become a nationally known Evangelist, and later had a weekly T. V. program. Talk about being in a shadow. To be fair, I would not have had much of a career in Christian ministry, if not for the many doors He would open for me.

I am among those who believe that God has a special purpose and plan for every human being. But it's up to us to respond to His presence and His call. I believe that, even at birth, He creates us with certain talents and strengths which, of course, have to be nurtured, developed, and used. The other day my dentist asked, "What do you think your God-given talent is?" Without hesitation, I said, "Encouragement". He agreed. How did I get from being too "bashful" to talk to anyone to being an "encourager"? It's simple. Just like everyone else, as I grew older, God revealed to me that I could do; what I liked; what my possibilities were, and how to get there from where I was. When I was very young, I would stroll through the field on our small farm singing, "Jimmy Crack Corn", which was a popular song at that time. But, you can be sure, I made sure no one could hear me. Or so, I thought. My brother John D, who was 14 years older than me heard me singing in the field. He was now in his twenties and making a little money. **So, he offered to pay**

me if I would sit on his knee and sing for the family. No way! That is, until he offered me money. Ten cents! That's more than I had. So I said, "yes."

HOW DID GOD HELP ME TO OVERCOME MY FEARS?

One of the things that happened to me, being so shy and insecure, was to become a loner. While my siblings and I did just about everything together, both work and play, I enjoyed going on walks in the forest by myself. But I never wanted to "stay" alone. I needed my family around me. To this day, I love my solitude. But I love people even more. **I was 12 when we moved to San Francisco. Even then, I would sometimes go for all-day walks into the dangerous, downtown area. I would just tell Mama that I was "going for a walk."** I'm sure she did a lot of praying until I got back. The other side of my personality had me delivering Daily Newspapers, riding a bicycle. My brother Grady also had a paper route with a different San Francisco newspaper. And, when I was in the eighth grade at James Lick Junior High School, I joined the School Safety Patrol, directing traffic on all the streets around the school grounds, even becoming the captain. We, the Safety Patrol, were once asked to participate and march in a City-wide parade held at the Kezar Stadium, later used by NFL teams. Although I didn't like San Francisco, I got a lot of experience there that helped me later in life. **The big city was not my thing, but God would later use my experiences there to put me into Inner City Ministry. Now, I love both the city - and the mountains.**

HOW DOES GOD PREPARE SOMEONE LIKE ME, SPIRITUALLY?

The wooded trail that our family took to church, almost two miles, was a perfect opportunity to practice my singing skills while, at the same time, keeping me enough distance from other family members so as not to be heard. Did I mention that, when I was very young, I saw myself, someday, growing up and doing something significant, like singing, that would encourage others? I wanted to "let my light shine." I would be in my second year of Bible College, taking a speech class, when it finally hit me, not only will I not pass the class if I didn't get over my shyness, I will never see my dreams come true. It was a "wake-up" call that changed my life. I became much more outgoing. **And I began to realize that my God-given purpose in life would include becoming a "people person."**

When I accepted Christ as Lord at a young age, I had a tremendous hunger for the Word of God, the Bible. We were given a New Testament at our church. So, my walks then became very special times of fellowship with God. I would stop, sit down and read - then pray. I would Pray - then read more. As a result, the Holy Spirit was so strong in my heart, I knew that my life's purpose would be to serve God, however He chose to use me. To this day, I love to take walks, and drives, to have special, personal times with the Lord. I believe that this is part of how the Lord prepares us for service, no matter what our beginnings may look like.

I truly enjoy talking with and challenging incarcerated teenagers to realize their "God-given" purpose in life. Most of them don't even know they have such a purpose. I believe God loves to take the least and the worst of us to demonstrate His power. He loves us so much and wants us to succeed. He wants us to have an enjoyable, full life. He never says, "I don't need you, or want you." And it doesn't mean that it will be easy, for any of us. In fact, the Bible says that, in Christ, when we are weak, then we are strong.

2 Corinthians 12:9-10 (NIV) But *he said to me, "My grace is sufficient for you, for my power is made perfect in weakness." Therefore, I will boast all the more gladly about my weaknesses, so that Christ's power may rest on me.*

10 That is why, for Christ's sake, I delight in weaknesses, in insults, in hardships, in persecutions, in difficulties. For when I am weak, then I am strong.

Every one of us has a story, a testimony, if we will but use it. God's plan is to use everything in our lives, even from birth, both the good and the bad, to bring glory to Him. **"Being me" should not be my goal in life, rather, "Glorifying God", the One Who made me, should be my desire and my purpose in life.** This is accomplished by turning everything over to Him. The Holy Spirit then turns everything into something useful for Him. Guaranteed!

WHO SAID, "HARD WORK NEVER HURT ANYONE?"

One of the things I often tell juveniles is, "You will never really be happy or successful until you learn the value, and joy, of hard work." In a time when so many are trying to "get out of working," we are missing one of the most essential elements of how God will work in, and through us, not only to provide for our family but also to be happy, and to be a blessing to others. I know that not everyone will even have the opportunity to work, let alone work hard. Whether it's manual labor, teaching, or long hours at a desk job, there's something fulfilling and satisfying in knowing you have given your best. Yes, some will become "work-a-holics," which is not good.

And some will neglect their families and loved ones in pursuit of personal gain. **On the other hand, being a "hard worker" will get you noticed.**

We, like millions of Americans, lived in the very difficult days of the Great Depression. Everyone was expected to work. No exceptions, except being physically or mentally unable. I still have vivid memories of "Chopping wood;" "Picking cotton;" and walking everywhere we went. Usually, the only meat we had with our meals came from hunting wild game, and fishing. What does this have to do with "Pure Religion?" **It helps if we have learned to "roll up our sleeves" and do whatever needs to be done. We are more likely to relate to people in third-world countries who have little to nothing, and who know the meaning of "hard work."** For them, it likely means survival. On my mission trips to the slums of El Doret, Kenya, I have seen hundreds of people who are walking the streets every day. I asked the Pastor, "What are they doing?" He said, "Looking for anything they can do to survive another day." Can you imagine trying to support a family like that? For them, it's reality. It's very tempting for them to abandon children, even babies, or to sell their children to "human traffickers." This puts things in a different perspective when it comes to us comparing our difficulties to theirs.

It's very important that we can look back and know that we have learned very valuable lessons stemming from our childhood, or difficult days in our past. Have we become hardened, or bitter, because we may have had a hard life? I'm not saying that being abused, abandoned, or terribly hurt in some other way, is a good thing. However, the Bible says that, for those who are His, God can, and does, take anything and everything and turn it into something good. Something that glorifies Him. **Romans 8:28 (NKJV)** *"And we know that all things work together for good to those who love God, to those who are the called according to His purpose."*

When we can say that we are "Blessed", it means that we have indeed, benefitted from our trials. Like someone once said, "Life is hard - then you die." **But, in Christ, we are not just "survivors," we are made, "more than conquerors" through Jesus!**

Romans 8:37 (KJV) *"Nay, in all these things we are more than conquerors through him that loved us."*

CAN I REALLY BECOME, "JUST LIKE JESUS?"

Lord Jesus, "Help me to see others today, as you do, and respond accordingly." Years ago, in my early morning, pre-dawn, walks, I started praying this prayer. Why? The Holy Spirit had already begun working in my heart to begin primarily, ministering to "down-and-outers." This eventually led to somewhat of a "Sea Change" in my ministry priorities. God was showing me that most of my life in ministry so far was mainly about my "career." It actually took some other things as well, setbacks in my life, to get me to start listening to Him. He loved me enough to allow some very painful failures that would get me to see what He wanted me to do. When we established Memphis Inner City Outreach in 1989, one of my best preacher friends said, **"Don, if there was a list of the "Ten people most likely to never start an inner-city ministry, you wouldn't even be on the list!"** Does that tell you anything about how I came across to some people? Still, I welcomed the challenge. I knew I was in for a blessing, if I didn't give in to my fears. I desperately wanted to leave my past behind, and to be Jesus to the hurting.

I knew I had my work cut out for me. And I definitely knew that God was leading me / us to do this, even though I wasn't exactly prepared yet, spiritually. So, my daily morning walks became "confession" time with God. "Lord, give me compassion - and humility." I knew that every promise of His was mine, that He would provide everything necessary, including a new attitude. And I knew I <u>was</u> going to follow through with this. **<u>No turning back! It would turn out to be one of the most important decisions I would ever make.</u>** And it became one of the most rewarding experiences of my life. I love it more and more every day!

IS THIS WHAT I WAS ACTUALLY MADE FOR?

Do you think that maybe everything that happens in our lives here on earth will, somehow, actually affect our eternal lives, once in heaven? I do. **Ephesians 2:10 (NIV) says, *"For we are God's workmanship, created in Christ Jesus to do good works, which God prepared in advance for us to do."*** Since God "worked" in creating us, He means for us to "work" with Him - now. He actually calls us, "Joint heirs, partners, with Christ." **Romans 8:17 (NIV) *"Now if we are children, then we are heirs—heirs of God and co-heirs with Christ, if indeed we share in his sufferings in order that we may also share in his glory."*** That won't stop once we get to heaven.

Work is not a dirty word. It suggests accomplishment, value, identity, and purpose. God is inviting us to do something very special with Him - and for Him.

Revelation 14:13 (MSG) *"I heard a voice out of Heaven, 'Write this: Blessed are those who die in the Master from now on; how blessed to die that way!' "Yes," says the Spirit, "and blessed rest*

from their hard, hard work. None of what they've done is wasted; God blesses them for it all in the end."

While we are being "prepared" for meaningful service in the here and now, God is using our experiences here to prepare us for an eternity of service in heaven. It will be anything but boring! **And, He is with us every day, making sure that we will have everything we need.**

WHAT'S IN IT FOR ME?

There is a whole world out there, begging for someone to be the hands and feet of Jesus. He worked tirelessly to serve others, while also demonstrating to us just how it's done. What awaits us are blessings, too many to count. If you've ever done something meaningful for someone else, something that truly blessed them, you know the "high" that it gives you. It is said best in **Acts 20:35 (NIV)** *"In everything I did, I showed you that by this kind of hard work we must help the weak, remembering the words the Lord Jesus himself said: 'It is more blessed to give than to receive.'"*

Thank you, God, for Your Son, Jesus, who gave His all for the likes of me, and for all mankind. Show me, every day, someone who needs the same love you have given me. "Pure, True, Religion." In His Name. Amen

SOMETHING TO THINK ABOUT:

When have I ever felt inadequate for something I had to do?

CHAPTER 8

"I AM BLESSED! - NOW WHAT?"

2 Corinthians 9:8 (RSV)
"And God is able to provide you with every blessing in abundance, so that you may always have enough of everything and may provide in abundance for every good work."

Ephesians 3:16-19 (NIV)
"I pray that out of his glorious riches he may strengthen you with power through his Spirit in your inner being,

17 so that Christ may dwell in your hearts through faith. And I pray that you, being rooted and established in love,

18 may have power, together with all the saints, to grasp how wide and long and high and deep is the love of Christ,

19 and to know this love that surpasses knowledge—that you may be filled to the measure of all the fulness of God."

WHAT DO YOU MEAN WHEN YOU SAY YOU ARE "BLESSED?"

"I won the lottery!" "My ship came in!" "You won't believe what just happened!" OK. What about all the people who can't say something like that? Are they not also, "blessed?"

One day, during the early days of Memphis Inner City Church, when we were still meeting in the renovated warehouse, a lady walked in and sat down while I was in the auditorium getting things ready for the Sunday service. It was very hot that day. A little overweight, she was panting and sweating, having walked from her home in the hot, humid, delta heat. I went over to say "Good Morning. How are you." **"I am blessed," was her instant reply. I'm thinking, "you can hardly breathe, and you're saying, you are 'blessed?'"**

That was over 25 years ago, and I still remember it like it was yesterday. As a matter of fact, a few years ago, I decided to say, "I am blessed" every time someone, anyone, asked me, "How are you?" I am "blessed" by most of the reactions I get, such as: "Aren't we all blessed?" "Blessed, and highly favored!" One day when I was on tour in Missouri on a Sunday morning, I stopped at a truck stop on my way to church to get a cup of coffee. An older teen-age girl waited on me. She didn't ask how I was doing, so I asked her first. She said she was "fine," "OK," like she wanted to be somewhere else other than working on a Sunday morning. Then, she asked me, "how are you?" I said, "I am blessed." Her response was, "Awesome!" Her whole demeanor totally changed! I have had literally hundreds of similar responses as hers. That's why I enjoy saying "I'm blessed," every time anyone asks. It immediately changes the atmosphere, and conversation. No, I don't start preaching to them. But it does open the door for them if they want to talk more, especially about how good God is, or what Jesus means to them. Sometimes people will open up about needing prayer for some special need they, or someone else, may have. **Another thing, saying, "I am blessed" doesn't offend anyone. It's not being "politically incorrect." However, it definitely implies something**

very spiritual, that "God is good," and, we are all "blessed!" We can be "thankful!"

IS SAYING, "I AM BLESSED," THE SAME AS SAYING, "I AM LOVED?"

If someone says, "I am blessed," you know they feel really good about something. In spiritual terms, I believe they are saying, "I feel loved." We are blessed, even when we have problems. There is joy. Circumstances don't change that. There have been times when I have been really frustrated about something, which often happens in airports, and didn't feel like saying, "I am blessed." But I would say it anyway. Guess what? It works! It helps to keep me from starting to complain to those around me. **I hate being negative, or irritable. I much prefer being a "blessing."**

I believe we are also talking about the grace of God. Unmerited favor. Undeserved love. It's only when we realize God's unconditional love - and grace - that we are confident that we are "blessed." We can have real peace. Peace that people don't understand.

This is a quote from a Dayspring card: *"Because of Jesus....we have peace that passes understanding. We have joy that can't be taken away. We have love that's everlasting. We have nothing to fear and everything to hope for today, tomorrow, and always."*

IS THERE ANOTHER DIMENSION TO BEING "BLESSED?"

Have you ever referred to someone as being "gifted," "anointed," or just plain "brilliant?" I think we all have met, or know about, someone like that. Praise God for such people. But there might be a couple of things to consider in reference to people who really stand out. First, are we using our talents (gifts) to glorify God or ourselves? Do we find it easier, or harder, to relate to those less outstanding? More importantly, as a Christian, am I more, or less, accessible to the poor, homeless, and so on? Am I more, or less, like Jesus? This is not meant to be judgmental, jealous, or envious of someone more "blessed" with talents than we are. But, simply to point out what often happens when someone becomes the focus of everyone's attention. **That person will be faced with the challenge of being "humble," Christ-like, and showing genuine love for others.**

If God blesses you with exceptional talents, even if you have worked really hard to accomplish your success, do you have any responsibility to be a "blessing" to others? **This is not referring to giving everything away - to people who just want "hand-outs."** It's about giving back your time, yourself, and what you have learned on your way to success. And yes, sometimes giving back financially to something you truly believe in. The problem I have seen so many times, especially in Christian circles, is a wider gap between our successes, and those God intends us to bless. When I had opportunities in years past to speak and sing at Christian Colleges, I would always try to make the point that God is preparing you to use your education, no matter how many degrees, and your "gifts," to serve others. Instead, we are tempted to use it to further a personal agenda, missing the blessing God had planned for us, and those He wants us to serve.

It really all comes down to humility. If anyone ever had any reason, or right, to boast, it was Jesus. He's the One I need to emulate. He gave up the glories of heaven to come and save me. What have I given up for Him? Am I willing to say to Him, "I am Yours. And all

66

that I have, all that I am, is Yours, not mine?" **Am I "blessed" with special gifts and abilities? God expects me to use such things to be a blessing to others - in the name of Jesus, and to God's glory! It won't get any better than that!**

"The higher I get up the ladder of success, the harder I must endeavor to bless those who are at their lowest!"

HOW CAN I SAY "I'M BLESSED" WHEN SOMETHING BAD HAS HAPPENED?

Many years ago I read Merlin Carothers' book, "Prison To Praise." It tells how he, himself, was incarcerated and how he began to "praise God" for his circumstances. It became his focus every day. When he was released from prison, he began a ministry to help others, like himself, to find that God does, indeed, work all things together for good in every situation, to those who are His. **For the rest of his life, he truly believed that his worst circumstances brought the greatest blessings from God.**

That was a tremendous help to me when we began to work in prisons, and with the homeless and poor in Memphis. To have confidence in telling them to "praise God, and thank God, in all circumstances, was saying to them, 'when you praise God', you bring Him directly into your situation." He's just waiting for us to ask for His help. **He's not trying to push us away. He's trying to get us closer to Him. He's saying, "There's nothing I can't handle."**

It's not to say that God deliberately brings hurtful things into our lives for no reason. However, whether He does it, or just allows it, He always has a blessing waiting for us. And, yes, He will at times allow the Holy Spirit to lead us into situations that are meant to be difficult for us. It was the Holy Spirit who led Jesus into the wilderness to be tempted by the Devil: **Matthew 4:1 (NLT)** *"Then Jesus was led out into the wilderness by the Holy Spirit to be tempted there by the Devil."* In my first chapter I asked, "Did God set me up?" Thank God, He knows better than I do what I need in my life. If it's a challenge, a difficulty of some sort, that will help me grow, then, whether I want it or not, I need it. We know that the storms of life bring hidden blessings and strengths. There are so many examples we all know of. I marvel at friends of mine who have suffered so much, yet still praise God, knowing that He has something far better in store. **I'm not going to ask for something bad to happen. Never. But, when it does, He promises to give me whatever I need to glorify Him.** He promises that, in heaven, we won't be disappointed: **Romans 8:18 (KJV)** *"For I reckon that the sufferings of this present time are not worthy to be compared with the glory which shall be revealed in us."*

WHAT DO MY TALENTS AND ABILITIES HAVE TO DO WITH "PURE RELIGION?"

Everything. **Colossians 3:27 (NIV)** *"And whatever you do, whether in word or deed, do it all in the name of the Lord Jesus, giving thanks to God the Father through him."* If I, as a Christian, do anything for any other reason, I am bringing glory to myself. And, if that's my motivation, I probably won't even go near the poor, whether here or in a foreign country. What would be the point? **The last thing I need to be doing is trying to "fool" others into thinking I'm something that I'm not. It won't take long for me to be exposed as a phony and a fraud.**

On the other hand, if I see my talents and abilities as opportunities to bless others, I will have a great time sharing and connecting with them. My experience in foreign countries has been that they don't judge you by whether you sing good or speak well, or better than someone else, but by your humility and sincerity. They know whether you want to be there with them, or not. It's really about "denying" self, and lifting others up. By the way, this is also true if, and when, you go to the homeless, or to prisons. I'm often asked, "What do you say to them?" "We'd like to do something like you are doing, but we just don't know how to go about it." If someone is sincere about wanting to do this, we will gladly train you and take you with us.

"A faith to live by, a self-fit to live with, a work fit to live for, somebody to love and be loved by - these make life."

"If we learn how to give ourselves, to forgive others, and to live with thanksgiving, we need not seek happiness - it will seek us." ...Joseph Fort Newton - Everyday Religion - Abingdon - Cokesbury Press

HOW HAVE YOU BEEN "BLESSED," AND WHAT ARE YOU DOING ABOUT IT?

I want to encourage you to start saying, "I am blessed," every time someone asks, "How are you?" Recently, I was in a church in Missouri to share Christ in word and in song, and an older man entered the building just before we started. **He said, "when you were last year, I heard you say 'I am blessed.' I want you to know that, ever since then, I have been doing the same thing. And, I'm so happy that I did. It has changed my life!"**

Didn't Jesus say to "let your light shine?" (Matthew 5:16) So, how do we do that, especially in places where you can't, or won't, talk about Jesus? It's very rare to hear anyone mention the name of Jesus in public, for fear of offending someone, or being ridiculed. That's certainly true in the U. S. But I can tell you that it's not that unusual in some other countries, like Africa.

It's not just about offending people. What about when Jesus said, "If you deny Me before others, I will deny you before My Father in heaven." Is He talking about not being willing to mention His name, Jesus, in public conversation? Ouch! How does that make Him feel? I'm just saying, "let's at least find a way to start that conversation." Maybe saying, "I'm blessed" will at least open that door. **Sally once said to me, "I heard that you can see a candle from ten miles away. Do you believe that?" "Only if it is lit," I said. Let's keep our candles lit.**

Luke 9:26 (NRSV) *"Those who are ashamed of me and of my words, of them the Son of Man will be ashamed when he comes in his glory and the glory of the Father and of the holy angels."*

Matthew 10:32-33 (NRSV) *"Everyone therefore who acknowledges me before others, I also will acknowledge before my Father in heaven;*

33 but whoever denies me before others, I also will deny before my Father in heaven."

Romans 1:16 (NKJV)" For *I am not ashamed of the gospel of Christ, for it is the power of God to salvation for everyone who believes, for the Jew first and also for the Greek."*

Lord may Your Holy Spirit strengthen me with humility, and boldness, to be a true witness for Jesus today. May others be "blessed" by being around me. In Jesus Name. Amen

SOMETHING TO THINK ABOUT:

In what ways have I been blessed the most?

CHAPTER 9

"PURE RELIGION" - WITHOUT GRACE?

Ephesians 2:8-9 (NLT)
"God saved you by his special favor when you believed. And you can't take credit for this; it is a gift from God.

9 Salvation is not a reward for the good things we have done, so none of us can boast about it."

ISN'T IT <u>ALL</u> ABOUT GRACE?

There's really no question that we cannot save ourselves. No matter what we do, we can never merit God's grace, His salvation. But we still keep trying. Someone has said, "we will never understand God's amazing grace, meaning His unconditional love, until we come to grips with the 'depravity' of mankind, including our own. Our unworthiness must finally hit us between the eyes! Then, and only then, may we begin to understand what God's grace means to us. Yes, every command of Christ must be obeyed. Still, it is only by His grace that we are saved.

I Corinthians 6:9-11 (RSV) *"Do you not know that the unrighteous will not inherit the kingdom of God? Do not be* *deceived; neither the immoral, nor idolaters, nor adulterers, nor sexual perverts,*

10 nor thieves, nor the greedy, nor drunkards, nor revilers, nor robbers will inherit the kingdom of God.

11 And such were some of you. But you were washed, you were sanctified, you were justified in the name of the Lord Jesus Christ and in the Spirit of our God."

I was brought up to believe that my salvation, and my acceptance into the body of Christ, was based totally on how well I was doing. From week to week, I might be lost or saved. Even when we "obeyed the gospel," there was the constant implication that my performance was the only measure of my having been "saved". There was such a strict code of conduct that sometimes made me dread having to live up to expectations set by others. I'm not talking about being faithful in Sunday School and worship services, helping others, growing in my knowledge of Christ, and living a good moral life. I'm referring to never being "good enough." And always being made to feel guilty about everything I did or said. Nor am I referring to God's command to be "holy," even "striving toward perfection." The difference is that it is God, in His grace, who helps me every day to accomplish this, not rules and expectations set by others. People, on the other hand, may try to use our imperfections to condemn and control, even after we have been "set free" in Christ. **I can guarantee you that freedom in Christ, knowing that you have been forgiven and your burdens have been lifted, is a lot more effective in your progress than responding to constant guilt.** Where's the joy in that? The Word of God says that I am now the "righteousness of God" - in Christ! Hallelujah!

2 Corinthians 5:21 (NIV) *"God made him who had no sin to be sin for us, so that in him we might become the righteousness of God."*

WHAT'S THE DIFFERENCE IN "GRACE," AND BEING "GRACIOUS?"

According to Webster: "Grace" - is "the favor and love of God." "Gracious" - means "to be pleasantly kind or courteous." It's the second part I want to talk about here.

When I returned from my first trip to Shillong, Meghalaya, India, I couldn't stop talking about how "gracious" the people there had been to me. Bana & Margaurite Uriah were my hosts for three trips. They have established a very successfull mission in the Jantia community. They went out of their way to please me, and to make sure that I had the best of everything that they had. I knew that they were very poor people, yet they "spared no expense" to show hospitality like I had never seen before. Why? Not because I was from the U. S., important, or to make a good impression on me. No, it was because of the love of Jesus in them. **Their love for the Lord was overflowing. I became the recipient of that love. Isn't this how we are to treat one another?** I have been blessed by so many wonderful people in my travels over the years, because it's who they are, people who love the Lord and who love to love others. I have been truly inspired by such gracious people.

Now, getting back to others' "rules and expectations." I have sometimes witnessed preachers and churches literally turn a "cold shoulder" to those who no longer meet their expectations. Since we began our Inner-City Mission, decades ago, I have had some churches, and ministers, where I once traveled in and out for years, not to allow me to come back, since I have worked with other churches and denominations. Some feel that I have become too liberal, too compromising. **One preacher even sent me a list of questions as to who I approved of, or not, from other churches, as though I believed exactly as they did.** One of my best friends of many years, a member of that congregation, had helped arrange for me to come back for a program. Then, when I got the minister's letter, along with a list of questions about my beliefs and associations, I wrote back, explaining that I was simply obeying the Great Commission - to "go into all the world." It doesn't say, "except, to certain other churches." Since I have been working with other churches, my beliefs have not changed at all. As a matter of fact, I have had many opportunities and open doors to preach and teach what I have always known from the Word of God. This is true in foreign countries as well. Anyone who works, or volunteers, in prisons, or foreign missions, knows that you are often expected to work with volunteers from other churches - without publicly criticizing them. In the prison system, it's the law. **It doesn't mean that we all believe or teach the same thing. But it does mean that we will be working together, respecting and encouraging one another, as we serve our Lord, Jesus Christ, together.**

It is sad to see the lack of grace in some who can't accept that there are those who differ from them. I have often listened to certain speakers who, in clinics and retreats, rant about others in their own fellowship, making differences of opinion a **"test of fellowship."** That's a term used to condemn others, and to refuse to work or even worship with them. I don't want to be guilty of judging others when they believe God has chosen to use them in a different way than me. Rather, I want to encourage them, and rejoice in what they are doing for our Lord.

There will always be opportunities to share with others and to discuss differences we may have. I have learned that just about every denomination has their own "good reasons" for not associating or working with others. Some are even worse than we are. It's also sad that we don't believe we have anything to learn from other churches. Seems pretty hypocritical, and unfortunate, to me.

How is it that some of us feel that it's ok to condemn others who are in the same fellowship as we are, calling them "unbelievers," having "forsaken the faith?" Isn't that being rather judgmental? How about "admonishing one another," as the Bible teaches us to do, instead, and not allowing our differences to so easily and quickly to divide and separate us? At some point it is perhaps a matter of power and control, motivated by pride! **Couldn't we show grace and humility instead? I am convinced that such negative attitudes and in-fighting severely weakens our influence for Christ in our communities, exposing our self-righteousness, even perhaps driving lost souls away.**

HUMILITY AND GRACE WIN - EVERY TIME!

One of the humblest men I have ever known was Lawrence Layman. He was the brother-in-law of our minister, Harold Dunson, whom I wrote about earlier. He was a true example of one who practiced "Pure Religion". He and Harold, along with their families, both moved to our neighborhood in Oklahoma about the same time. Brother Layman worked tirelessly with the Kiamichi Mountain Christian Mission in its early days, and for decades to come, when so much needed to be done raising funds; establishing churches, and promoting the annual Kiamichi Christian Men's Clinic, which drew thousands of men from all over the U. S. He was a great encouragement to me in my first years in Ministry, including ordaining me into full time ministry. His son, Mark, and I were students at Midwest Christian College in Oklahoma City at the same time, and often commuted together to preach in churches back near our homes, almost 200 miles one way. There were times that Mark and I hitch-hiked to and from college, together, before either of us had a car. We remain good friends to this day.

I am so thankful, and blessed, to have had such men as Lawrence Layman and Harold Dunson, as mentors and examples of humility, integrity, and grace. I have endeavored to use what they taught me, both in ministry and in training others. Because of them, I learned first-hand the true meaning of "Pure Religion."

IS GRACE A DUTY OR A COMMAND?

Short answer: yes. I don't consider fellow believers to be my "enemies," but sometimes these are the hardest to love. That's why there is so much teaching in the Bible about loving, and demonstrating love and grace, to other members of the body of Christ.

Romans 12:3 (NIV) *"For by the grace given me I say to every one of you: Do not think of yourself more highly than you ought, but rather think of yourself with sober judgment, in accordance with the measure of faith God has given you."*

Romans 12:10 (NKJV) *"Be kindly affectionate to one another with brotherly love, in honor giving preference to one another;"*

Galatians 6:2 (KJV) *"Bear ye one another's burdens, and so fulfil the law of Christ."*

Sometimes you just have to surprise someone with an "act of kindness." Say something encouraging. Do something they don't expect - from you. If people don't respond, or don't seem to care, don't stop doing "acts of kindness." Continue to be a "blessing." We may be unaware of difficulties others may be having at the time. Some may be carrying negative memories that continue to affect their lives. Maybe they just don't like you. Can you handle that? Remember, it's not about you - or me. It's about responding to everyone, and every situation, as Jesus would, with love and kindness. **Sometimes it's as simple as being the first to say, "Hi. How are you?" Then, when they say, "Fine. How are you?" You say, "I am blessed! Thank you for asking."** Remember the Golden Rule? **Matthew 7:12 (MSG)** *"Here is a simple, rule-of-thumb guide for behavior: Ask yourself what you want people to do for you, then grab the initiative and do it for them."*

ISN'T GOD'S GRACE AMAZING?

Grace is grace. That's why you can't fake it. You can pretend to be "nice," but people will see through it, quickly. Neither is there such thing as "Pure Religion" without grace, unconditional love that knows no bounds. Don't you just love people who "love people?" They are magnetic. We want to be around them. We admire, and even envy them, wishing we could "love like that." **I can just picture Jesus, smiling, laughing, while at the same time, genuinely asking others, "How are you doing?" Everyone liked him, loved him.** Except, of course, people who didn't like anybody, and those who were jealous and envious of Him. These are the same ones who just wanted to get rid of Him. He threatened their "Power base." Pretty much what still goes on today.

AREN'T WE SUPPOSED TO BE "EMISSARIES" OF GOD'S GRACE?

Just take a look at those who were prominent in the New Testament: Paul, Peter, John, James, and of course, Jesus. It was grace, the unconditional love of God, that was demonstrated, attracting people from every nation to something they'd never seen before. Now, this is our job, our responsibility. Let's take it to the poor, the broken, and to the downhearted. Let's take it to those in prison; those in third-world countries; to China and Russia; to Europe and Middle eastern countries; next door; down the street; in the mall**. Be different. Be a blessing. People will notice, especially our Lord Who is cheering us on!**

1 Peter 2:9 (NKJV) *"But you are a chosen generation, a royal priesthood, a holy nation, His own special people, that you may proclaim the praises of Him who called you out of darkness into His marvelous light;"*

2 Corinthians 5:18-20a (NLT) *"All this newness of life is from God, who brought us back to himself through what Christ did. And God has given us the task of reconciling people to him.*

19 For God was in Christ, reconciling the world to himself, no longer counting people's sins against them. This is the wonderful message he has given us to tell others.

20 We are Christ's ambassadors, and God is using us to speak to you."

Precious Lord God, make me an ambassador for Jesus, demonstrating His love and grace to everyone I meet today. May my love for you, Jesus, be most important - in my quiet place, my work, and in my daily living. In Your name, Jesus. Amen

SOMETHING TO THINK ABOUT:

What is my understanding of the grace of God?

CHAPTER 10

"AM I MY BROTHER'S KEEPER?"

Genesis 4:9 (NIV)
*Then the LORD said to Cain, "Where is your brother Abel?" "I
don't know," he replied. "Am I my brother's keeper?"*

AM I MY SISTER'S KEEPER?

It seems to be mostly in poor, third world countries, but not
exclusively, that small children, even babies, are neglected or even
abandoned, by their parents. Often, it will then fall on siblings, many
who are still children themselves, to care for them.

Our family of eleven, nine boys and two girls, were pretty much like
most other families we knew, a little abnormal. But, since we didn't
know it at the time, it didn't matter. Being the last of the bunch, I
have to say that, for my entire life, I have been treated very well by
all my brothers and sisters. Every one of them have done so many
things for me, many times, sacrificially and generously. Our parents
were from the "Old School," not much on mushy words, but very
heavy on loving through actions. **I honestly do not remember
either of my parents ever saying, "I love you." But, boy, did they
ever show it!** I don't ever remember going hungry, or being ignored
when sick. Daddy always made sure that we each had gifts under the
Christmas tree every year, even when work was scarce, and funds

were low. While we did go through a lot of "hard times," we were truly loved by our parents, and by each other.

I can't resist telling a story or two about my siblings, the ones closet to me in age. When my sister, Josie and I were maybe 4 or 5 years old, we decided to build a fire - under our house! We were bored and looking for something to do. Our house was built on a slope, so the front porch was a few feet off the ground, making it easy to crawl under the house. There were plenty of dry sticks under the house, so with a match, we easily got the fire started. Thankfully, someone saw what we were doing and quickly put the fire out - as well as my sister and me! **One other time, we plucked the feathers off of a chicken, while it was still alive! We thought seeing a "naked" chicken would be kind of funny.** I guess we figured that the chicken, sooner or later, would be eaten. The only reason we had chickens was for eggs, and eating. So why not go ahead and get it ready? Since I was the youngest, I told everybody it was Josie's idea to do these things. I keep reminding her of that whenever I stay at her house when I'm in the area where she lives. She's still looking out for me.

IS THERE ANYTHING WORSE THAN NOT CARING FOR YOUR OWN FAMILY? 1 Timothy 5:8 (NLT) *"But those who won't care for their own relatives, especially those living in the same household, have denied what we believe. Such people are worse than unbelievers."* It's very clear that God expects us to care for our own families. There's no "Pure Religion" without it. However, perhaps, in our hearts and minds, we need to extend the boundaries of our families to include those "abandoned" or "orphaned," no matter how far they live from us. **My recent trip to Zambia clearly brought this up front and center to me. I could no longer tell myself, "They aren't really my family.** So, I'm not obligated to help them. If it's convenient, yes, but it's not my responsibility. They will be ok without me." Jesus might not see it that way.

Apparently, "caring for orphans and widows in their distress" is the highest level of service that the Lord wants us to be aware of. A lot of things matter in life. But, if this is not at the top of our list, something's wrong. Shouldn't we pray and ask God to give us the same love for others, even strangers, that we give to our own families? Maybe that's what He's trying to get us to see and to understand. Then, perhaps our outlook, and outreach, would include everybody. **We could actually go looking, every day, for someone who needs a blessing. Just like Jesus.**

DID MY SISTER HELP ME A LITTLE TOO MUCH?

When I was in the second grade, Josie was in the third grade. I was falling behind. So, she helped me catch up. She did such a good job that I was promoted from the second grade to the fourth grade, skipping the third grade. Thank you, Josie! But then she failed the third grade and had to take it over, putting me ahead of her, since I had been moved ahead while she had fallen back. I don't think she was so happy about that. She will tell me, "I helped you and look what it got me!" But when we were in Junior High School, we returned from San Francisco to our home school at Nashoba, and she was moved back up even with me, and we graduated in the same class. **If she had it to do over, would she still have helped me when I was in the second grade? You'll have to ask her. She was just looking out for her little brother. I will remain forever "grateful."**

DID I TAKE ADVANTAGE OF MY BROTHER?

When we lived in San Francisco I turned 13 years old. And, since it was such a long bus ride to school every day, I thought, "If I had a really good bicycle, it would be much easier to get to school and back home every day." By now, my brother Lee had graduated from High School in Oklahoma, and returned to San Francisco and was working at the U. S. Post Office there, saving money to go to college. So, I told him my idea about buying a bicycle to ride to school, but that I didn't have the $40.00 to get it. That was a lot of money in 1953. He did loan me the money to get the bicycle. I really don't remember how he felt about it, but it seemed like a good deal for me. So, the next day I mounted my new, ten-speed bike and rode all the way across San Francisco to my school. Now, since bicycles were not allowed inside the school, I had brought a really good chain and lock, parking it right in front of the school, with the chain around a light post. When I got out of school in the afternoon - it was gone! I've already written about how backward I was. **So, I walked all the way home and didn't say a word to anyone about the bike being stolen. I pretended that nothing had happened!**

The next day, when I arrived at school, my new bicycle was right back where it had been stolen from the day before! Not only were my prayers answered, but whoever had stolen the bike apparently was told to "take it right back!" Thank you, Jesus! I don't remember when, or how, I told my family, especially Lee, what had happened, I just know I was saved from terrible embarrassment. Lee, about four years older than me, was just looking out for me. Thank you, Lee! He has been not only a great brother and friend, but also a wonderful partner in ministry, as we have worked together many times in special meetings for the Lord. Do you think I have any excuse for not helping others in their distress, or, of demonstrating "True, Pure Religion," after what my siblings have done for me? (By the way, Lee says that I did repay him for the bicycle.)

DON'T YOU KNOW, I WAS TERRIFIED WHEN I REALIZED I HAD ALMOST KILLED ONE OF MY OTHER BROTHERS?

Grady, three years older than me, and I did a lot of things together, including squirrel hunting. So, when our "hunting dogs" treed a squirrel, running it up to the top of a very large tree to hide from us, we had a "sure-fire" plan to flush him out so that one of us could shoot him. I had my 12-gauge, long barrel, shotgun ready to shoot, when Grady, who was standing on the other side of the tree, directly opposite me, said, "There he is, on your side." **So, as I began to raise my shotgun, it accidently went off, just a few feet above Grady's head! I just missed him! I don't think Grady ever knew how terrible I felt, how shaken I was, almost killing him.** I have never forgotten it! Grady and I have had many wonderful times together in Christian ministry. Thank you, Jesus, for not allowing such a terrible thing to happen!

Grady has had to retire from actively ministering to churches, due to health reasons. He is one of the hardest working ministers I have ever served with. Now, he always wants me to know that he is praying for me. **The one thing he wants me to know most, which he has said to me many times in person, is this, "I love you, Don."** Sometimes he will repeat it, "I love you, Don". Hearing him say this means so much to me.

"BUT WHAT IF I'VE BEEN ADOPTED?"

Praise God, there are so many opportunities today to adopt a child and welcome him or her as a member of your own family. There are many being adopted from foreign countries as well. Have you heard the saying, and I believe it's true, "To be adopted is to be special, because you are deliberately chosen." This is exactly how God feels about us!

Ephesians 1:5 (NLT) *"His unchanging plan has always been to adopt us into his own family by bringing us to himself through Jesus Christ. And this gave him great pleasure."*

Galatians 4:4-7 (NLT) *"But when the right time came, God sent his Son, born of a woman, subject to the law.*

5 God sent him to buy freedom for us who were slaves to the law, so that he could adopt us as his very own children.

6 And because you Gentiles have become his children, God has sent the Spirit of his Son into your hearts, and now you can call God your dear Father.

7 Now you are no longer a slave but God's own child. And since you are his child, everything he has belongs to you."

In every foreign country where I have taken mission trips in recent years, we have invited people to help us raise extra funds to support orphans. Sometimes there are Orphanage facilities. Sometimes, as in my recent trip to Zambia, it will perhaps just be a community of orphaned and abandoned children. A lot of them. We have also supported orphans in China - multiple times. These children are at the mercy of those who are supposed to be caring for them. It is truly a joy to see and meet these precious children, and to leave something for their special needs.

When my son, David, was in the sixth grade I did a concert at his school. When he came home after school that day, he said, **"My teacher said, 'you sure look like your dad, even your hands'." He added, "I didn't have the heart to tell her that I was adopted!"** David is about six inches taller than me, so we don't actually look like each other. Besides that, he's a lot more fun-loving than me! And, he has brought so much pride and joy to my life, his "Pops," as he calls me. When David was about 14, he said, "I'm never having kids!" Of course, he now has a family of his own.

"ISN'T REAL FAMILY ABOUT RELATIONSHIPS - CLOSE TIES?"

Growing up, our family was actually pretty normal, in most ways. We worked and played together. We argued and complained a lot. We didn't talk those "mushy" words to each other, even though we were a very close family. However, since becoming adults, we have learned to say, "I love you," a lot! We have annual family reunions that have drawn us much closer to each other than we had ever been before. Every family has some members who are more successful or talented than others. That's to be expected. But all family members need all the others as well. The stronger ones should help the weaker ones, without making them feel like failures. And it's ok if the weaker one's "brag" about a brother or sister who is doing well. Ideally, we should always be looking out for each other. It is unfortunate, and sad, to sometimes see families who are not close. They may even be "estranged," having been hurt, or disappointed with some their relatives and not interested in going to their own family reunions. Sibling rivalries often turn into jealousy, and in some extreme cases, hate. **I believe God's plan is for our family**

units to be a major source of our earthly joy, even preparing us for life in heaven.

WHAT IF YOUR ONLY HOME WAS IN A GRAVEYARD?

One of the hardest things for a homeless person to deal with is not having a family or a place to call home. One of the members of our worship team at Memphis Inner City Church often told what really got him serious about getting off the street. During his days in Florida, he would watch people at the end of the day going to their homes for the night. "It began to hit me hard to realize that I had no home to go to." "Sometimes I would even look for a place in the graveyard to bed down for the night." Eventually he wound up in Memphis where the Holy Spirit led him to the Memphis Union Mission. As he renewed his faith in Christ, he began to get his life back, including a good job at a local music store. When I met him, we were needing someone with his musical talents to be a part of our worship team. He became a valued member of our staff for several years.

NO HOME? NO FAMILY?

Even Jesus was homeless while on earth, and his family (siblings) thought He was "crazy." "He's out on some ridiculous mission," they thought. He experienced lonely separation from his own family, just because they didn't understand or accept Him. He embarrassed them. **We found the homeless we met and helped on the streets of Memphis to be so very grateful that we would pay them any attention or help them.** Loneliness can be very hard to deal with. Let's remember that, instead of just judging and condemning the homeless for "getting themselves in a mess." In God's eyes, is their mess any worse than our own?

Luke 9:58 (NIV) *Jesus replied, "Foxes have holes and birds of the air have nests, but the Son of Man has nowhere to lay his head."*

WHAT IS GOD'S PLAN FOR THE HOMELESS, ORPHANS, AND WIDOWS?

To be sure, He does not ignore nor neglect them. **While we "look the other way," God is inviting them over to His house!** **Psalm 68:5-6 (MSG)** *"Father of orphans, champion of widows, is God in his holy house.*

6 God makes homes for the homeless, leads prisoners to freedom, but leaves rebels to rot in hell."

JUST WHO ARE WE, REALLY, IN GOD'S EYES?

One of my favorite sermons to preach is: **"My True Identity In Christ,"** something I need to be reminded of, often.

In Christ I am:

FORGIVEN (ACCEPTED)

RECONCILED TO GOD (RESTORED)

A NEW CREATION (NEW LIFE)

A JOINT HEIR WITH CHRIST (A PARTNER WITH GOD)

ADOPTED AS GOD'S CHILD

GOD'S AMBASSADOR

DESTINED TO BE LIKE JESUS

You have to admit, that's a pretty high position for any of us. Tell this to someone in prison, or homeless. You might have to do a little convincing. After all, they've always been told just the opposite - many times by us!

"Pure Religion"? Lord, open my eyes, more and more, to see what you see - in myself as well as others. In Jesus' Name.

SOMETHING TO THINK ABOUT:

How important is family to me?

CHAPTER 11

"AM I A 'FRIEND OF SINNERS?'"

Matthew 11:18-19 (NIV)
"For John came neither eating nor drinking, and they say, 'He has a demon.'

19 The Son of Man came eating and drinking, and they say, 'Here is a glutton and a drunkard, <u>a friend of tax collectors and "sinners."</u>' But wisdom is proved right by her actions."

Luke 15:2 (NKJV)
"And the Pharisees and scribes complained, saying, 'This Man receives sinners and eats with them.'"

JUST WHO ARE THESE "SINNERS?"

There are at least two categories of "sinners." We usually think of people who are "drunkards," "thieves," "liars," or maybe, "rapists, and murderers." They are, for sure! But, what about Jesus befriending despised "Tax-Collectors," or people who are simply mean, "losers," failures in life? Do we find ourselves "bending down" to their level in order to help them, and to love them? Even the most devout church members have trouble with these. We usually won't even give them the time of day. It would be beneath our dignity. Our church is better than that. We are better than that!

See why we have a problem with being a "friend of sinners?" Are we still talking about "Pure Religion?" Isn't this supposed to be about those who can't help themselves, what has happened to them? Not what they have done to themselves?

ARE WE ALSO SUPPOSED TO TREAT "BORN LOSERS" THE SAME WAY WE WANT TO BE TREATED?

When Daddy and Mama moved out of our "Old Home Place," a homeless family wanted to rent the house. Daddy told them, "You can move in, at no cost, for as long as you need to." For many of us, our parents had learned lessons of life the hard way, through many personal difficulties. Looking out for neighbors was automatic - for most people. They passed on to us important values like honesty; integrity; hard work; and, caring for those less fortunate.

Although Mama served the Lord, diligently, for her entire life, Daddy was not a religious man. He had many very good qualities, but being spiritual was not one of them. That is, until he gave his heart to the Lord, at age 64. Even though he now had four sons in the ministry, plus other children serving the Lord in various ways, he was holding out. **Then, one day when our brother Cecil came home in between his travels doing revivals, Daddy, sitting on the front porch, said, "Do you think I could be baptized today?"** It shocked all of us! It seems that the Holy Spirit had been working in him to bring him to this point of surrender. Daddy was always a proud man. So, this was a defining moment for him.

WOULD OUR "SWIMMING HOLE" NOW BECOME A BAPTISTRY?

We were all pretty excited about what was going to happen next. We walked, about 300 yards, to the place where, for many years, we would swim, bathe, and fish, to witness Daddy being baptized into Christ. As Cecil led Daddy into the water, Lowell Mason, Cecil's song evangelist, and a great Todd family friend, sang, "I'd Rather Have Jesus." Don't know how many "tears" were shed that day, but our hearts were truly humbled at what we witnessed.

Why is this story important? Daddy had always had a big heart. Now, he would be so - as a Christian. One side note: **Daddy gave all of us kids "nicknames." He nick-named me "Donkey." It was the only name he had ever called me. That is, until he became a Christian. Then, he began to call me by my given name, Don**. And he began to show a new side of himself, one of humility. I was a student in Bible College at the time, coming home on weekends to preach at a Choctaw Indian Church at a nearby community called, "Divide," meeting in an old school building. He insisted on going with me every Sunday, as I drove the few miles from our house to the church. He was happy, and I was very proud of him, and proud to be his son - Don. Much of whatever I have learned about loving the "unlovable," I learned from him.

HOW DID WE AVOID, OR SURVIVE, SNAKE BITES, AND MOUNTAIN FALLS?

Was God there with us - all the time - from the beginning? It has taken me, personally, quite a long time to really begin to understand what was going on as we were growing up. Praise God, we were all exposed to the Word of God, a Church family that cared for us, a strong Christian mother, and a sense of God's blessings - every day. (I now know that His blessings were revealing His over-all purpose for the rest of our lives.) No, everything wasn't perfect, but there was a "bond of love" that permeated everyone, and everything around us. **I tell juveniles in detention, "God created you, uniquely, for a**

91

purpose. You are not here by accident. Your birth may have been unplanned, or even unwanted, but it is God who made you. Only one you. Don't you want to know why?"

I also tell people everywhere I go, locally or internationally, that the God who made you, made you for a purpose - to glorify Him. And, as a Christian, Jesus Christ, through His Holy Spirit, is with you - always! You are never alone! When we know this for certain, we are free from self to worship and serve the Lord, and to do great things for Him.

WHAT IF I'M NOT "OK" WITH LOVING "REALLY BAD" PEOPLE?

What about people who have hurt other people, terribly? A lot of names come to mind. Shouldn't they be shunned, since they have done so much harm? Jesus knew that we would face the same kind of people He faced, "enemies!" "LOVE YOUR ENEMIES?" Are you kidding? Do we mean it, even if we say we do? Isn't God's love "unconditional," making no distinction? Can we pray, "Love, through me," "Bless, through me?" He knows that we do not have it within ourselves to love our enemies. That's why He told us what to do. Call on Him. Admit that we can't - on our own. Our love for Jesus, who has forgiven us, the worst of us, should compel us to do whatever pleases Him, even loving our enemies. **Where would the Apostle Paul be without the forgiving love of Christ? He would still just be "Saul of Tarsus, murderer!"** Isn't love stronger than hate? I choose love! We are not condoning any wrong anyone has done,

but doing what is 'impossible with man, but possible with God." "Pure Religion." Works every time!

Donald W. Todd

DOES THIS MEAN I CAN FINALLY "GET OUT OF THE BOX?"

Why are we so bound by "being what we have always been?" Is it because most people let us get away with it? Should it take some kind of "shake-up" in our lives to jar us out of ourselves? I dare you. Do something good, that no one would expect you to do. Some people would be "surprised" if you spoke "kindly" to them. Why? Because you are not expected to. It doesn't always have to be someone you think is below you. Start greeting people whom you think are better than you. Do it with grace, and humility, not expecting something from them. **Do we limit what the Lord wants to do in, and through, us? Go ahead, be a "blessing" to someone today!**

ARE YOU TELLING GOD, "I JUST CAN'T?"

"I can't be a 'friend of sinners.'" "I can't go talk, and pray with that person." "I can't go on that mission trip." "I'm not a "Super Christian." "I just can't forgive him / her." "I won't let bygones be bygones!" As a Christian, you and I no longer live. We have "died with Christ." He dwells in my heart - by the Holy Spirit. The following Bible verses have helped me many times:

Philippians 4:13 (NKJV) *"I can do all things through Christ who strengthens me."*

Colossians 3:3 (MSG) *"Your old life is dead. Your new life, which is your real life—even though invisible to spectators—is with Christ in God. He is your life."*

Colossians 3:12-14 (NIV) *"Therefore, as God's chosen people, holy and dearly loved, clothe yourselves with compassion, kindness, humility, gentleness and patience.*

13 Bear with each other and forgive whatever grievances you may have against one another. Forgive as the Lord forgave you.

14 And over all these virtues put on love, which binds them all together in perfect unity."

Hebrews 2:9 (NLT) *"What we do see is Jesus, who 'for a little while was made lower than the angels' and now is "crowned with glory and honor" because he suffered death for us. Yes, by God's grace, Jesus tasted death for everyone in all the world."*

It's also important to remind ourselves that Jesus said, *"Yes, I am the vine; you are the branches. Those who remain in me, and I in them, will produce much fruit. For apart from me you can do nothing."* **John 15:5 (NLT)** So, clearly, it's not me, but Christ in me. Praise the Lord!

IS THIS WHY JESUS WAS LOVED SO MUCH?

Well, not everyone loved Jesus. There were people who despised Him, and wanted Him to just "stay out of their way." But, to others, He was such a "breath of fresh air," compared to the pretenders and religious leaders who were "abusers" of God's people. He was "irresistible" to those who were drawn to Him and believed in Him. The more they got of Him, the more they wanted. **When you and I truly represent Jesus to others, especially those who don't expect it, we are always in for a special blessing. He will make sure of it.**

John 1:11-12 (NKJV) *"He came to His own, and His own did not receive Him.*

12 But as many as received Him, to them He gave the right to become children of God, to those who believe in His name."

"Settle this in your mind, that your salvation consists in expressing the nature, life and Spirit of Christ Jesus in your outward and inward new man. Put priority on those things which exercise and increase the Spirit and life of Christ in your soul, and that contribute toward changing you into the likeness of Christ." ....
The Inner Chamber - Andrew Murray - CLC Publications - Fort Washington, PA 19034

EVER WONDERED WHY THEY DIDN'T "PICK" YOU?

Remember your childhood games at school? We can understand why team leaders and captains would want to choose only the "best" ones available for their teams. They want to win. I can remember being left out, not "chosen," a lot of times. I also know how it made me feel. Sometimes I just gave up and went and did something else. Other times, however, it made me want to work harder, so I would eventually make the team. That can be very healthy and good for your self-image and your progress, if you are not too hard on yourself.

The problem in life, however, is that we may begin to feel like even God has overlooked us, that He has more important people, and more important things to do, than to pay attention to us. That can hurt more than anything else. How do we fix that? We who are God's people must always be aware that people are looking at us, and, based on our actions, whether we accept them or not, it is really God, accepting them or not accepting them. We may not like it, but that's the way it is. We are His voice; His eyes; His ears; His hands and feet; His heart. **Everything we say and do should reveal who Jesus is to the world today. Who else is going to do it?** This is our assignment. It's who we are. I want to remember this in the context of practicing "Pure Religion." I don't want to be hypocritical, nor biased, when paying attention to those around me. There are a lot of hurting people needing someone to love them with the love of Jesus. I want them to see "Jesus in me."

ISN'T THIS WHAT YOU AND I WOULD RATHER BE?

Make me a blessing, Make me a blessing,

Out of my life - may Jesus shine;

Make me a blessing, O Savior, I pray,

Make me a blessing to someone today.

Copyright 1924 - <u>George S. Schuler Copyright 1952, Renewal. The Rodeheaver Co., owner</u>

I praise You, Lord Jesus, for loving me, choosing me, and using me, to bring glory to God, our Father. In Your Name, Jesus. Amen

SOMETHING TO THINK ABOUT:

When have I ever felt left out and did not matter?

CHAPTER 12

"GLORY TO GOD!" OR "GLORY FOR ME?"

Galatians 6:14 (KJV)
"But God forbid that I should glory, save in the cross of our Lord Jesus Christ, by whom the world is crucified unto me, and I unto the world."

ARE WE GUILTY OF ROBBING GOD OF HIS "GLORY?"

Of course, we are. From the day of our birth, we have literally been "crying" for attention! We learn how to get what we want, and how to avoid what we don't want. We devise schemes and methods to not just "survive," but how to win over those around us. This can be either healthy, or selfish. As we develop our strengths and skills, we may begin to assert control over others, including siblings. **Sooner or later, we may begin to use others, or even to abuse them, to get what we want. Eventually, it will affect our professional lives, and unfortunately, our Christian witness and relationships.**

It can come down to "taking credit" for what someone else does. Or we may sabotage someone else's accomplishment to make it our own. There are a lot of ways to be deceptive in order to make ourselves look better. There are countless examples in the Bible of someone taking advantage of someone else, regardless of what it meant to the one being taken advantage of. There are Biblical examples of individuals who blatantly declared themselves to be some kind of "God!" **The real God always found a way to reverse whatever was happening so that no one ever survived such an idiotic assumption!**

I think some of the worst offenders now, in our modern day and time, are those who feel that they know more than God, that they are better than God, and that they certainly are not "accountable" to God for how, or what, they do. We think ourselves more capable than the God of the Bible, of "judging" what is right or wrong, or even who should, or should not, go to heaven.

How many of us actually expect that we, or someone else who has lived an extraordinary life, should be rewarded, applauded, or "recognized," for our earthly accomplishments, when we get to heaven? Yes, the Lord himself will say to those who are His, "well done, good and faithful servant," but no one, no matter who we think is deserving, will be worshiped or receive glory, except, our Lord, Jesus Christ! End of discussion! **Can you imagine anyone getting to heaven and trying to get special attention? If we were going to pick someone, anyone, where would we even begin? And yet, that's what we are doing now, every day!**

WILL IT ALWAYS BE THIS WAY?

Let's face it. Since mankind fell from the grace of God in the Garden of Eden, the human race has shown a real problem with pride. As it was "hatched" from the Devil himself, it continues to permeate just about every area of our lives. Even Christian people must deal with pride, and with the difficulty of denying self, even for the sake of our Lord, Jesus Christ. It seems that we are "wired" toward "looking out for number one," first and foremost. And, when we are challenged to own up to our "Self-Righteous" attitudes, we pretend to be shocked, and deny any such thing exists. **I can tell you for sure, I am among those who must deal with pride every day. Unless I quickly take responsibility in every situation, as soon as I realize that pride and self-centeredness are rising up, I must take it the Lord - in prayer, or, it will just quickly get worse!**

I can think of at least a couple of scenarios where pride seems to thrive. If our goal in life is to be "rich and famous," or, even just "famous," we might be in for some terrible disappointments along the way. If success is my primary goal, I am likely to be using people and situations only for what they can do for me, discarding those who don't fit into my personal goals and ambitions.

BUT WHAT IF SUCCESS COMES BECAUSE I'VE EARNED IT?

That would be great! However, the real question is: How do I handle "Success?" Do I begin to look down on others, those I don't think are as successful as I am? Does my success make me more, or less, accessible and tolerable of others? Even as a Christian, does my life, and walk of faith, draw me closer to others? Or does it make me feel "superior" to them? Yes, success may mean that we don't have as much time to give to others, due to schedules and responsibilities. But, does that mean that we can't still be caring and helpful, showing the love of Christ to everyone? **People can read our "body language" and know whether we care about them or not.**

For the first several years when I would speak to groups of teens in detention at Juvenile Court, I would tell them that I believe their main purpose in life should be to "make a difference," for good. A lot of examples came to mind: there may be some urgent need in their neighborhood where they could be useful; or a cause for which they could offer themselves, their time or abilities; or, even to take a mission trip, perhaps to a third world country, somewhere where they could truly make a difference. There is almost always a positive response to the idea. But, actually doing something about it upon their release means to make a serious commitment to helping others, not self. It would mean facing their own failures, in order to be prepared to help others.

ISN'T THERE A "HIGHER CALLING," THAN JUST SELF ACCOMPLISHMENT?

I have since changed my mind about what I tell them. Now, I tell incarcerated young people that I believe their purpose in life is to "Glorify God," the One who made them, "In His image." You can do that no matter what your life's goal or ambition may be. **To please God means to surrender everything in your life to Him, that He will always come first**. There may be times when you might even fail, lose everything, and have to start over. That shouldn't change your relationship with God, your heavenly Father. If you keep your trust in Him, He will never fail you, leave you, nor forsake you!

Doing good things that make you "feel good," doesn't necessarily mean you are doing what God wants you to be doing. It may mean that we are just really enjoying the response we get from helping others. It's actually better than any artificial "high" you might be getting. And you are to be commended for "doing good." But who's getting the glory?

SHOULDN'T I BE HELPING OTHERS INSTEAD OF HELPING MYSELF TO THEM?

If I really want to glorify God and not self, won't I be looking for opportunities to help them, instead of using them? Isn't there someone who needs correction or encouragement? Someone I can humbly and gently reach out to, offering to lift his or her load? There may be a lot of people who may not be convinced that I actually care for them or anyone other than myself, until they see me, consistently loving and helping others.

Galatians 6:2-4 (NLT) *"Share each other's troubles and problems, and in this way obey the law of Christ.*

3 If you think you are too important to help someone in need, you are only fooling yourself. You are really a nobody.

4 Be sure to do what you should, for then you will enjoy the personal satisfaction of having done your work well, and you won't need to compare yourself to anyone else."

Acts 20:35 (NKJV) *"I have shown you in every way, by laboring like this, that you must support the weak. And remember the words of the Lord Jesus, that He said, 'It is more blessed to give than to receive.'"*

WHERE WOULD WE BE, IF NOT FOR NEW MUSIC?

Praise God for new music, new songs, in our worship services! I believe we should always be writing and singing new music. Every generation can make a very important contribution to improving and enhancing our worship through new music. The debate seems to be, to what extent are we willing to make drastic changes? Some churches are totally wed to the music of the past, not allowing anything much in the way of new music. Other churches are totally committed to nothing but new music - with a new style. When there is a stand-off, it may mean that pride is involved. I've seen churches lose many life-long members because new church leaders decided that nothing but new music, in the new style, would be permitted. I have even had someone literally "cry" on my shoulder, as she left the building, citing the loss of the worship music she had always known. But, she was not yet willing to give up her church. I don't know about you, but this breaks my heart! **Is there not a common ground, along with the desire to please God, by ministering to everyone in the service through worship music? To humbly ask God for wisdom would surely make a huge difference in some of these situations.**

I am very much aware of how important it is to reach a new generation who do not relate to the older music. They have not had the experience that others have lived with through their hymns over their lifetime. However, would it not be to the benefit of the younger generation to learn and, hopefully, love many of the old songs that have meant so much to their seniors? Does it have to be either or? **Would the seniors (anyone over 50) actually be more receptive to new songs, new music, if they felt that they were not being ignored? Instead of anxiety and disappointment, might there be peace instead? What is more fulfilling than a whole auditorium of saints singing, joyously, to the Lord?**

Just try to get a crowd out on a Sunday night, unless they believe it will be even more entertaining than whatever else is going on at home, or somewhere else. I have had a music ministry for many, many years. I certainly want to do well - very well, to be as professional as I possibly can be. And I will be the first to tell you, I am somewhat "out of date!" Not what you would call, "Entertaining!" If I am still doing music for myself, for my own success, who do you think I'm wanting to be glorified? Me first. God second. When people do offer compliments, what should be my response? **If I don't give God the glory, humbly, it means that I want it for myself.**

BUT WHAT IF I CAN'T AVOID THE "SPOTLIGHT?"

Praise and adoration can be very "Intoxicating!" Even if you think you've earned it. It seems that we have been, for quite a long time now, in a culture that expects to be entertained, even in our churches. There has been a tremendous shift in the style of worship in our church services in recent years. One of the hottest, ongoing debates has to do with styles of worship music: Contemporary - or Traditional, which do you prefer? Change can be good. Very good. Each new generation, including this one, is far advanced from the previous generation in many areas. It is reasonable that those changes would affect our styles and methods of sharing the gospel. It does, however, require a strong foundation, and wisdom, to make changes successfully, without sacrificing others in the process. It is often heard, "You can't argue with success." It usually refers to growing larger churches. While that's a very good point to make, **every decision to**

make changes must be only after much prayer for the Holy Spirit to give us wisdom. So much is at stake! Much knowledge requires much wisdom. And, greater talent begs greater humility!

If God puts me in a position of being in the "Spotlight," how does it look to Him if I have taken the glory for myself? I can tell you, "It's very tempting to do just that!" Applause can feel really good. But then, what do I do to recover from getting a lot of attention? I must spend extra time, in private prayer and worship, admitting and confessing my unworthiness, repenting and apologizing to the Lord for taking His glory for myself. This is mandatory for me**. I would caution anyone who is in the spotlight, singing or speaking, to be aware of who is getting the glory, Jesus, or me?**

HOW CAN WE TURN A NEGATIVE INTO A POSITIVE?

I actually believe that the Holy Spirit can, and will, take a subject like this (self-centeredness) and turn it into something good. How? I am learning more and more every day how essential it is, first thing every morning, in my private place and time with the Lord, to ask Him to be Lord of my life and King of my heart today - all day. But we know that it's no time at all until things start to fall apart. **It's like the flesh, self, is saying, "wait a minute! I'm still in charge here!" I have to say, "NO, you are not!" "I am a child of God. Jesus lives in me, and He is Lord of my life!" This is "Spiritual Warfare!"** It goes on all day, every day. That's why the Lord's word says, *"Pray without ceasing!" 1 Thessalonians 5:17.*

Luke 9:23-24 (NKJV) *Then He said to them all, "If anyone desires to come after Me, let him deny himself, and take up his cross daily, and follow Me.*

24 "For whoever desires to save his life will lose it, but whoever loses his life for My sake will save it."

Galatians 2:20 (NIV) *"I have been crucified with Christ and I no longer live, but Christ lives in me. The life I live in the body, I live by faith in the Son of God, who loved me and gave himself for me."*

Let's keep it simple. Be a servant, not a "glory seeker." Make it your goal every day, to seek out others who need a blessing. Ask God to lead you in the path of someone in need, a need God can use you to fulfill.

CAN I BUY YOUR BREAKFAST?

The other day I stopped at a fast-food restaurant to get coffee on my way to the Post Office. Inside, I saw someone curled up in the seat of a single booth. Head was down but I knew it was a woman. While I was drinking my coffee, she was putting her coat on, getting ready to leave. She looked over at me and said, "Haven't I seen you at the Union Mission?" I said, "Yes." Then she said, "Didn't I used to see you years ago at the downtown Memphis Inner City Church?" Again, I said, "Yes." She said, "I used to attend your church, years ago." Then, knowing she was homeless, I said, "Can I buy your breakfast." "That would be nice," she said. "What would you like," I asked. "Pancakes," she said. I took her to the counter, ordered pancakes, coffee, and more. As I was paying with cash, she said, "could you give me the change for bus fare?" (She could get an all-day pass for $2.50) "Of course,". **I think sometimes Jesus is saying to us, "Do you really want to spend more quality time with Me? This is where I'll be, with those in need."**

As I left and continued on with my day's activities, I was feeling truly blessed, knowing that God had answered my prayer to help someone that day. He also answered her prayer for something, someone, to keep her going for another day. We had a special time, rejoicing in God's goodness!

Lord, God, thank you for showing each of us just how easy it is to be a blessing to someone today, while at the same time being blessed! Pure Religion. In Jesus' name. Amen

SOMETHING TO THINK ABOUT:

Do I find that I'm sometimes wanting glory for myself, that should belong to God?

CHAPTER 13

HOW IMPORTANT IS THE BIBLE, THE WORD OF GOD, IN MY LIFE?

2 Timothy 3:16-17 (NKJV)
"All Scripture is given by inspiration of God, and is profitable for doctrine, for reproof, for correction, for instruction in righteousness,

17 that the man of God may be complete, thoroughly equipped for every good work."

Hebrews 4:12 (NKJV)
"For the word of God is living and powerful, and sharper than any two–edged sword, piercing even to the division of soul and spirit, and of joints and marrow, and is a discerner of the thoughts and intents of the heart."

HOW I LEARNED ONE OF THE GREATEST LESSONS MAMA EVER TAUGHT ME!

I don't know how I missed it all those years. I was over 40 years old when I learned that Mama had been reading through the entire Bible - every year! I thought she would have been way too busy to have the time necessary to do something like that. She had raised eleven children in very difficult times, and was constantly keeping in touch with all of us, including dozens of grandchildren. **When she had a heart attack in her 70's, it took about six people to cover the things she had been doing each week in her home church in Clayton, Oklahoma.**

Most people, possibly over 90 percent of steady, church-going, Christian people, have never read through the whole Bible. I had been to Bible College, had been in ministry for over 20 years, and still don't remember ever reading through the entire Bible, cover to cover, except perhaps as a required assignment in a college class. **Now, after learning that Mama took the time, every day, to read the entire Bible every year, I had no more excuses. I had to follow her example. It literally changed my life.**

HOW IMPORTANT IS A "CLOSE," PERSONAL RELATIONSHIP WITH THE LORD?

I had been brought up reading the Bible - Old and New Testaments. However, it was basically "head knowledge." "Bible Drills," seeing how fast you could find Scripture: Book, Chapter and verse, before someone else could, was an exciting exercise when we were kids. Many of our church youth groups participated in "Bible Bowl," which involved competition with other youth groups, locally and nationally, to see who was best at learning and knowing the Bible. The best ones would be invited to compete for the first prize trophy at an annual Christian Convention. The whole process can be not only exciting, but also great for kids getting to know the Bible.

While it is very important to become familiar with all the books of the Bible, and to be able to turn, quickly, to any given text, it is then up to each of us, as individuals, to allow God's word to touch our hearts and change our lives. This takes commitment and discipline, and desire. **What I don't remember, as a young person, was anyone really encouraging me to develop a deep, personal relationship with the Lord, which meant daily, private prayer and worship.** I'm sure it was implied by our Minister, and teachers. But it was also assumed that, if we knew the Bible, could even "quote" a lot of Bible verses, that all was well. Even today there are many who believe that's all we need to do. I believe that this is one of the reasons why many Christian teenagers, upon leaving home, also lose interest in church attendance and Christian living. If there has not been a developing, close relationship with the Lord, and His word, the Bible, there is no longer a foundation upon which to stand or grow in the faith. There are many who feel that today's universities and colleges are the worst places for a Christian young person to go. Sometimes it is true even of Christian colleges. **Even the strongest young believer is going to meet opposition, temptation, ridicule, and trials, like they have never seen before! It is up to the individual to make sure that the Lord comes first, no matter when or where.**

WOULD I BE ANY DIFFERENT THAN ANYONE ELSE?

Just as God is no "respecter of persons," neither is the Devil. Nearing mid-life, I found myself facing some very difficult challenges. Even after many years of serving the Lord, I knew that my relationship with the Lord was not as close as it once was. Keeping busy, working for the Lord, doesn't necessarily mean staying strong in the Lord. It is too easy to think, "It's all about me: my career: my happiness. Putting self-first even resulted in a broken marriage. This allowed me to look into my heart and ask, "What is really important to me?" **Through those years, with God's help, and the Holy Spirit leading, I began to rebuild my life, putting the Lord first where**

I had been putting self-first. I not only was now reading through the Bible every year, I also developed a routine of early morning "Prayer Walks," beginning around three a.m. I realized that, unlike so many people, **God is in the business of "rebuilding" and "restoring," our lives, rather than "discarding."**

Mama's example and prayers never stopped. She would write, faithfully, words of love and encouragement. In one letter she wrote, "Remember, you are a preacher!" It wasn't just reading the Bible more, it was applying God's Word to every area of my life. This was certainly what I needed during difficult personal times, and for what was to come next. **In just a few short years, Sally and I would be launching our Inner-City Mission in downtown Memphis. God had also been leading her to new and very different avenues of service.**

JUST HOW IMPORTANT IS "DAILY BIBLE READING?"

One very significant outcome of my reading through the Bible every year resulted in the Lord leading me to write, "Daily Praises," a daily devotional that guides the reader into every chapter of every book of the Bible, including reading through the Bible in a year. It emphasizes the very personal relationship we need with the Author of the Bible, our Lord, Himself! We simply must have the daily, one-on-one, contact that includes reading, listening and, praise, and worship. He longs to be not only our heavenly Father, but also our dearest Friend! **In just about all of my talks I encourage this close, personal relationship with the Lord, including daily Bible reading, first thing in the morning.** Not everyone will have the same opportunities, or be in convenient situations, as in prisons, or homeless, but all can start the day with the Lord. And we can all learn from the example of others, including our mothers, how to draw closer to God.

*"The life that with wholehearted devotion gives up all for God and to God can also claim all from God. Our God longs exceedingly to prove Himself the faithful God and mighty helper of His people. He only waits for hearts wholly turned from the world to Himself and open to receive His gifts." ...**Andrew Murray - The Ministry of Intercession***

HOW DOES PRACTICING "PURE RELIGION" BEGIN?

It should, of course, begin when we are young and learning all about God, Jesus, and the Bible. However, for many of us it doesn't seriously begin until God has allowed something very traumatic to happen in our lives. I believe God used everything in my life, right up to mid-life, for something far greater than I had ever dreamed. My first mission trip was to Haiti in 1986. I have now made seven trips to Haiti, most recently with, Djumy Septembre, who is now a dear friend, founder of CARHA - Christian Action and Relief for Haiti. **Haiti is a wonderful place to minister to orphans and widows, practicing "Pure Religion." All third-world countries are mostly populated with the "very poor," with many opportunities to serve those most in need.**

I can remember well my first Haiti mission trip. I traveled with a group associated with Northwest Haiti Christian Mission, going to the northern border towns and cities. Compared with the other team members (over 20 of them) I was somewhat "spoiled," since I had been traveling in full-time evangelism for almost 20 years, being treated "royally" everywhere I went. There was plenty of work for all of us to do. In fact, I had never seen so many hundreds and hundreds of people needing food, clothing, and medicine. I was so moved by my interpreter that I left him all of my clothes, except what I had on, when we left to return to the U. S. I was truly inspired and motivated by the Haitians' love for the Lord, and their humility during times of worship and praise. Their hunger for the Lord has made a lasting effect on me for the rest of my life. When we returned to the U. S., it was total "Culture Shock," for me, realizing the difference in what I had always known as my Christian life, now compared to the Haitians. **For at least six months, everywhere I went to sing, preach, or visit, I tried to make everyone feel guilty for not being more like the Haitian Christians, or not also going to Haiti as I had done.** I know that was very insensitive on my part. But I just couldn't remain the same as I had been before going to Haiti.

I will confess, shamefully, that I thought I had so sacrificed of my time and self, that I actually told people, "I don't ever plan to go back to Haiti!" "I love them, but I don't want to go back." Why? "Too hard on me!" "Too difficult!" I even told some, "The best view of Haiti for me was, "looking down from the window-seat of the airplane as we flew back on our way home, away from Haiti!" You would think that I would have had a more "spiritual" reaction to all that I had experienced, especially getting to know and be with the wonderful Haitian Christians. However, in a few weeks, after I got over my "jet lag," it really began to set in, what a blessing it had been to go there. **On my next record album I included a song about my experience in Haiti, "On A Carribean Island," to let people know just how much it meant to me. It was a front-row seat to experiencing "Pure Religion."**

SHOULD THE BIBLE AFFECT ALL OF US THE SAME WAY?

This chapter is about the importance of God's Word in our lives. It doesn't just "save" us, it also directs us how-to live-in ways that please God. I think that pleasing God is more than reading the Bible more. We have to take His Word more personally, as the Bible teaches.

James 1:22 (NIV) *"Do not merely listen to the word, and so deceive yourselves. Do what it says."*

- Charles Haddon Spurgeon (1834-1892) "Oh, to be bathed in a text of Scripture, and let it be sucked up in your very soul, till it saturates your heart!

- Dwight L. Moody (1837-1899) "The Bible will keep you from sin, or sin will keep you from the Bible!"

- A. W. Tozer (1897-1963) "The Word of God well understood and religiously obeyed is the shortest route to spiritual perfection. And we must not select a few favorite passages to the exclusion of others. Nothing less than a whole Bible can make a whole Christian."

I have been known to offend at least a few people over the years, usually when I have spoken at conferences, by emphasizing that I don't believe we should hide behind our Bible doctrines, or our Bible knowledge, as good as it might be, so that we don't feel any real compulsion to go and serve the lowest of society. It doesn't seem to be essential to our salvation, or getting to heaven. Why would a majority of us, with a few exceptions, not do what God says about reaching out to the poor, the prisoner, or the homeless? Are we missing His special blessings when we don't go to them?

Perhaps we don't trust God to protect us, or use us, like He might do for someone else going into difficult places. How do we know that God won't just leave us on our own to fend for ourselves? There's an Old Testament King, Asa, King of Judah, to whom God sent the prophet, Azariah, with the following message:

2 Chronicles 15:1-2 (NIV*) 1 The Spirit of God came upon Azariah son of Oded.*

2 He went out to meet Asa and said to him, "Listen to me, Asa and all Judah and Benjamin. The LORD is with you when you are with him. If you seek him, he will be found by you, but if you forsake him, he will forsake you."

Doesn't this mean that God is with you and me also? We are, like Asa, in a spiritual battle, a battle for the souls and lives of everyone! We won't get any closer to God, or be used by God, any more than when we are deep into His Word, and in prayer, every day. Again, it's not me, nor you, but Jesus inside our hearts, who wants to use us to do His great work today.

JUST THINK!

You're not here by chance,
but by God's choosing.
His hand formed you
and made you
the person you are.
He compares you to no one else -
you are one of a kind.
You lack nothing
that His grace can't give you.
He has allowed you to be here

at this time in history
to fulfill His special purpose
for this generation.

.... Roy Lessin - DaySpring co-founder

Father, I have no greater joy than to know You, to walk with You, and to know your Son, Jesus Christ, as my Lord and Savior. I gladly spread His good news - the gospel that saves. In His name. Amen

SOMETHING TO THINK ABOUT:

Am I happy with my Bible reading, and, if not, what can I do to improve it?

CHAPTER 14

"WELCOME! - HOLY SPIRIT - COME ON IN."

John 14:16-17 (NIV)
And I will ask the Father, and he will give you another Counsellor to be with you forever—

17 the Spirit of truth. The world cannot accept him, because it neither sees him nor knows him. But you know him, for he lives with you and will be in you.

John 14:26 (NIV)
But the Counsellor, the Holy Spirit, whom the Father will send in my name, will teach you all things and will remind you of everything I have said to you.

HOW MUCH DO WE REALLY NEED TO KNOW ABOUT THE HOLY SPIRIT?

The Holy Spirit is both one of the most important subjects in the Bible, and one of the most misunderstood and confusing subjects of the Bible. Some prefer to focus on the theological aspect of the Holy Spirit: Who is He? Others focus on the special "gifts" of the Spirit, meaning, miracles and manifestations. Others may be more interested in what the "Baptism of the Holy Spirit," or the

"Anointing of the Holy Spirit," means. I believe much division has occurred, unfortunately, in the Body of Christ, as a result of positions taken with both of these approaches. **<u>Perhaps nothing is more important, and essential, than to understand the "Indwelling" of the Holy Spirit, as the very presence of Christ in us.</u>** In Acts 2:38, we are each promised the "gift" of the Holy Spirit upon our acceptance of Christ as Lord, and our obedience to Him. The entire book of Acts is also seen as the "Acts of the Holy Spirit."

WHY IS THE "FRUIT OF THE SPIRIT" SO IMPORTANT?

Paul writes in the book of Galatians of the "Fruit of the Spirit." If we desire to be like Jesus, is this not a true and accurate description of Who He really was, and is now also? And, if we ask, "What Would Jesus Do?" is this not the answer? Is this not crucial if we are to minister to those most in need - practicing "Pure Religion?"

Galatians 5:22-25 (NLT) *"But when the Holy Spirit controls our lives, he will produce this kind of fruit in us: love, joy, peace, patience, kindness, goodness, faithfulness,*

23 gentleness, and self-control. Here there is no conflict with the law.

24 Those who belong to Christ Jesus have nailed the passions and desires of their sinful nature to his cross and crucified them there.

25 If we are living now by the Holy Spirit, let us follow the Holy Spirit's leading in every part of our lives."

For myself, I am finding, more and more, that I have a desire to know the "Person" of the Holy Spirit. How does He relate to my day-to-day living? What does He *want* me to know about Him? I suspect that many people only know enough about the Holy Spirit to be very confused, and perhaps, discouraged. He may seem to be just some kind of mystical, ghostly presence. However, even the description(s) given by Jesus of the "coming" Holy Presence tell us so much more. We do know for sure that He is the third Person of the Trinity, equal in every way. He is: God - the Holy Spirit. He is the Spirit of the Living God. He is: Jesus - the Spirit of the resurrected, glorified Jesus, now sitting at the right hand of the Father - interceding for each of us, His followers! **He is the "Spirit of the Holy One of Israel!" He does not replace Jesus in me, but rather, "reveals" Jesus to me.**

Isaiah 45:11-12 (NIV*) "This is what the LORD says—the Holy One of Israel, and its Maker: Concerning things to come, do you question me about my children, or give me orders about the work of my hands?*

12 It is I who made the earth and created mankind upon it. My own hands stretched out the heavens; I marshalled their starry hosts."

HOW CAN THE HOLY SPIRIT BE "UP CLOSE AND PERSONAL" TO ME?

Rather than attempt to explain, or define, the Holy Spirit, as there are volumes and volumes of studies already available, I want to share how I believe He has been "up close and personal" to me in many ways. In so doing, I want to encourage others to take the same approach, to acknowledge the very presence of God, the Father, and of Jesus, God's Son, our Savior, through the indwelling presence of the Holy Spirit. To put it another way: the Holy Spirit only does or says what Jesus has given to Him; and, by the same token, Jesus does and says only what the Father gives to Him. **There is a constant, unbroken connection of Father, Son, and Holy Spirit, working**

in and through us, to bring glory to God, as well as God's blessings down to us. And, one more point, the Holy Spirit never contradicts what the Word of God, the Bible, has already given us. That's why it is so important to read, study, and know the Bible for ourselves. When there are differences as to interpretations of Scripture, the Holy Spirit will, in time, reveal the truth to us - when we ask! After all, He is the "Spirit of Truth." This re-enforces the need to be a constant student of the Bible in order to know its contents, and truths! **2 Timothy 2:15 (KJV)** *"Study to shew thyself approved unto God, a workman that needeth not to be ashamed, rightly dividing the word of truth."*

I will also add that, to me, the Holy Spirit has truly become my constant "Companion." He reveals Jesus, not Himself, to me in every situation. Every morning I invite Jesus, through the Holy Spirit, to be Lord of my life and King of my heart! **The Holy Spirit enables me to live for Jesus and to be Jesus in every situation. People will then see and hear Him instead of me.**

IS THE HOLY SPIRIT AN "INTRUDER"?

No, I must invite Him in. How do I know that? **Revelation 3:20 (NKJV)** *"Behold, I stand at the door and knock. If anyone hears My voice and opens the door, I will come in to him and dine with him, and he with Me.*

The Holy Spirit, Jesus, simply asks to be "invited." Is that not what we are doing when the Bible says to, **"pray** *without ceasing?"* 1 *Thessalonians 5:17 (KJV)* One of my favorite exercises is to invite Q & A during my Leadership Conferences in foreign countries. After each session I invite anyone to ask questions, on any subject, preferably about the lesson. I do not dare do this without first praying for the Holy Spirit to give me wisdom, and to lead and guide me in answering every question. Does this mean that whatever my answers are that it is automatically what God wants me to say? Not necessarily. But, when I ask, in Jesus' Name, He is not going to ignore my request. I have to say that this is so enjoyable, so enlightening, that I make it a priority. We usually spend as much time, sometimes more, in this participation of Q & A, than in the lesson itself. I find that the openness and honesty that is allowed is viewed by the attendees as a very beneficial exercise. Some of the questions are very basic, such as: "If I go to speak at a church, are they responsible for paying me and providing housing?" Answer: "If they invited you then you should have a mutual agreement, in advance, of the terms of your appearance. If you invited yourself, they are under no obligation to provide for you. Although, if you proved to be beneficial to them, they most likely will provide for you, and, may even invite you back." Could I have given that answer - without asking the Holy Spirit for wisdom? Yes, I can always "wing it," and do or say whatever I want, but, if I do, I will be giving "my" opinion, man's opinion, rather than "waiting on the Lord" for His wisdom and guidance. They don't need my opinions. They need to hear from God.

At this same conference one of the Pastors said, "I know there are some in the conference who believe they have the gift of healing." Then he added, **<u>"I have sometimes seen someone placing their hand on the head of the one being prayed for, then pressing down so hard, it's like they're going to break the neck! Is that necessary?"</u>** (We had just been studying Acts, chapter 3, where it records that Peter and John had participated in the healing of the man who had been lame from birth.) My answer: "It says in the Bible that 'he (Peter) took him by the right hand and lifted him up.'" (vs 7) This indicated that it was In the name of Jesus Christ of Nazareth, that he was able to 'rise up and walk!'" Healing was not in the men, nor the method, but in the power of Jesus' name.

I have found that allowing the audience, or class, to ask questions, or to make comments, also works very well in prisons, Juvenile Court, and even at the homeless shelter. Would it not be a great idea to allow at least a little bit of Q & A in some of our churches, during or after a sermon? Too much, you say? How else will you know if they are "getting" what you are "saying," unless they at least have an opportunity to have something explained or clarified? **Isn't the idea to adequately communicate the message to the listener? Yes, it would require a real desire on the part of the church and its leadership for it to work.**

HOW CAN THE HOLY SPIRIT LEAD IF WE DON'T GIVE HIM THE MICROPHONE?

In over 17 years of church services at Memphis Inner City Church, we got "burned" just a couple of times when we allowed "open mike" time. Even then, it is only necessary to be prepared in case someone takes too much time, or says something that needs correcting. However, **the blessings we received from hearing someone give a testimony, a prayer, a praise, or a song, were truly amazing!** I believe that the Holy Spirit will honor and bless the church that allows people, sometimes even strangers, to share something on their heart that is meant to bless others.

DOES THE HOLY SPIRIT ACTUALLY TELL ME WHAT TO SAY?

John 16:13-15 (NIV) *"But when he, the Spirit of truth, comes, he will guide you into all truth. He will not speak on his own; he will speak only what he hears, and he will tell you what is yet to come.*

14 He will bring glory to me by taking from what is mine and making it known to you.

15 All that belongs to the Father is mine. That is why I said the Spirit will take from what is mine and make it known to you."

Yes, He often tells me what to say. I once was talking to a preacher friend who told me he had just been with some of his friends who told him that God speaks to them, every day. He was very troubled, to put it mildly, that anyone would claim that God "speaks" to them! What audacity! He expected me to agree with him. My response, however, was that while I may doubt that God speaks to us, "audibly," I believe that He does speak to us - in our hearts and minds. Even if someone tells me that God has spoken to them, "audibly," I just say, "Praise the Lord!" **Who am I to tell them that they are lying, or exaggerating? That's between them and God. I believe that the Holy Spirit is constantly "speaking" to us. It is up to us to listen, and obey.** Oh, and again, I must remember that the Holy Spirit is not going to tell me to do or say anything that contradicts what the Bible teaches; that Jesus is with me at all times, giving me wisdom in every situation, leading and guiding me in important and serious matters. This may include everything from losing my keys, to what to say when sharing Christ, or counseling someone in spiritual matters. Thank you, Holy Spirit!

Matthew 10:19-20 NIV) *"But when they arrest you, do not worry about what to say or how to say it. At that time you will be given what to say,*

20 for it will not be you speaking, but the Spirit of your Father speaking through you."

That worked not only for the early disciples, it will work for you and me today. I can't imagine getting up in the morning, preparing to go through another day, and not praying first - about everything. I will have decisions to make, relationships to nurture, and challenges to face. Do I trust myself enough to ignore the Holy Spirit's leading - on everything? No, but I know I can trust the Holy Spirit for whatever I will need. It is imperative that I submit to His indwelling presence, for He represents Jesus in me. **The Holy Spirit prepares and enables me to "bear much fruit," bringing glory to the Father, in the name of Jesus. Again, He will not intrude, nor force me to do anything. He simply waits for me to ask for His help. When I do, He immediately goes to work in me, and through me into the world around me. That's Who He is; that's what He does!**

ISN'T "PURE RELIGION" JUST BEING OBEDIENT TO THE HOLY SPIRIT?

The most important, life-changing, decisions of my life came at the leading of the Holy Spirit. After going to Bible College for a couple of years, I had already accumulated debts I was unable to pay. Add to that, I also married much too young, unprepared for the responsibilities it would mean. So, I spent the next two years working in California in order to pay off my debts and to make plans to resume my college education back in Missouri.

While preparing to return to the Midwest, I was invited by my brother, Cecil, to travel with his evangelistic team during the summer, to be responsible for driving the semi-truck, plus, organizing area ministers and churches who would be participating in the crusades. Near the end of the summer, we were in Norton, VA, for a crusade to help get a new church "off the ground." Then, the small Norton church group asked if I would come back at the end of the summer and help them continue to establish the Norton Church. I did. And, to this day, I know it was the Holy Spirit that led me in this decision. The Norton church is still going strong, over 50 years later.

So, after a three-year delay, I made plans to leave the Norton Church in order to resume my college education. Again, my brother, Cecil, asked if I would spend another summer as his driver and organizer for his crusades. I accepted. Then, as summer was coming to an end, I was approached by a pulpit committee from a church in Amelia, Ohio. They had come to attend our crusade in nearby Kentucky, and to talk to me. They told me, "Our church is asking you to be our next full-time minister." They had recently experienced a bitter split that had so divided the church, they knew it was going to be very difficult to find another qualified minister to serve them. I accepted. Although I was there for only one year, it was a tremendously successful ministry. To this day, I still have very close friends as a result of that ministry. However, this time, instead of making plans to return to finish my college education, I had by now made so many friends while working with ministers and churches, through traveling with my brother, Cecil, that I launched my own music and preaching ministry. I would begin a life-long traveling, evangelistic ministry that would fulfill the dream of my childhood days, traveling for the Lord. I have no doubt that it was the Holy Spirit Who led me all the way. **This resulted in over 20 years of full-time evangelism. And, it laid the groundwork for establishing the special inner city mission in Memphis, where we have been now for over 30 years. Thank you Holy Spirit!**

I firmly believe that it is the Holy Spirit Who makes me aware of how important it is for me to look beyond myself and more to the needs of others. It is the Holy Spirit Who prompts me to deny self and to seek to reflect the Person of Jesus Christ to others, near and far. In all my previous years of ministry, He also was preparing me to travel into many foreign countries, sharing the gospel of Christ, and fulfilling the Great Commission!

WAS IT THE HOLY SPIRIT, OR JUST ME, MAKING DECISIONS?

As for my college education, I continued to take classes wherever I could, over the years. With one college, I even came to within one exam, plus one more three-hour class, to earn a degree. However, I completely lost interest, as it meant being identified with a school that I disagreed with, philosophically, and spiritually. I have not regretted that decision. Thank you, Holy Spirit. **My, "honorary" Doctor of Divinity degree is sufficient. I will always have more than enough opportunities to do what I love best. Thank you, Jesus!**

Whether I have been in foreign, third-world, countries, with the homeless, or with those in prison, rarely does anyone ask about my education. What is important to them is what I do, and what my attitude is around them. We cherish our times together, learning to care for each another. And, of course, for others. "Pure Religion," it happens!

Thank you, Father, for the path you have put me on. I wouldn't change a thing! Hallelujah!

SOMETHING TO THINK ABOUT:

How do I know that the Holy Spirit is living in me?

CHAPTER 15

IS IT TRUE - "LOVE NEVER FAILS?"

1 Corinthians 13:8 (NKJV)
"Love never fails. But whether there are prophecies, they will fail; whether there are tongues, they will cease; whether there is knowledge, it will vanish away."

1 Corinthians 13:13 (NKJV)
"And now abide faith, hope, love, these three; but the greatest of these is love."

How does an orphan know if he or she is truly loved? How does a widow, or a single mother, know if they matter? There may be a huge difference in the life and circumstances of someone living in a destitute, third-world country, as opposed to someone in the depths of one of our major inner cities. Some of us have had the privilege of seeing both situations firsthand. Is "being loved" any different, depending on the circumstances? Probably not. Hate and neglect, love and care, know no bounds. **You and I have marveled at those who have truly made a difference, such as George Mueller, who cared for thousands of orphans in the 1800's. Likewise, today there are many great and wonderful orphanages, both in the U. S., and in foreign countries.**

I HAVE NEVER BEEN LOVED MORE THAN IN CAMBODIA!

Some time back, perhaps ten years ago, we made orphans a priority in making foreign mission trips. We asked others to give extra funds to support orphans and orphanages in every country where I traveled. Sometimes there would be no actual orphanage facility, just abandoned children living on the streets, as I encountered in Zambia. In China, the government controls the care of orphans, and the elderly. But, they do it in their own way, without the influence of the Christian church. However, we found that, in many cases, churches choose to be involved in the government controlled orphanages by providing for the children, even assisting in the process of arranging adoptions. At one prominent orphanage, we delivered our financial gift, met all of the children and the staff as well. We were told that many of these orphans were being adopted, and that 80 percent of the adoptive parents were from the U. S. **I owe a debt of gratitude to Chuck & Helen Todd, World Mission Alliance, for opening doors for me to travel to China on mission trips.**

WHAT'S GOING ON IN CAMBODIA?

I thank God for the opportunities I have had to work with very special men and women of God who are rescuing, and providing for orphans in places like Haiti and Cambodia. I made my first of five trips to Cambodia with brother Joe Garman, founder and Director of ARM (American Rehabilitation Ministries) where Rapha House was established in 2005. It is now being led by Joe's daughter, Stephanie Freed. Rapha International has expanded in Cambodia, as well as into Thailand and Haiti. Some of the most wonderful times in my entire life and ministry have been with the children at Rapha who were "rescued" from "human trafficking." **I have never been loved**

more than by these Cambodian children! It was overwhelming! After my first trip to Cambodia, I told Sally, my wife, "I didn't want to come back home." That's how their love for me, just one of the volunteers, affected me. It was because of brother Joe Garman that I was able to make several trips to India. No place on earth is more in need of caring for "orphans and widows," than in India.

WHY WOULD I EVER WANT TO GO BACK TO HAITI?

I have also been amazed at the care for orphans I have witnessed in my trips to Haiti. In an earlier chapter I mentioned going to Haiti in 1986 with a group led by Northwest Haiti Christian Mission. It was a trip that had a huge impact on my life, and my ministry priorities. **In 2001, I met Djumy Septembre, a young Haitian Minister, who had come to Memphis to complete his Bible college studies. He and I became very good friends**. We invited Djumy to speak at our downtown, Memphis Inner City Church. He was well received as he shared about his Haitian homeland, and his goals for his people in Haiti**. His mission, Christian Action and Relief for Haiti (CARHA) is celebrating 20 years of service, reaching the very poor people of central Haiti**. I have been blessed to travel to Haiti to work with brother Djumy on numerous trips. I am seeing first-hand the rescuing of families, orphans, and the elderly, as churches, schools, and orphanages are being established. My activities also include "Leadership Conferences," as a part of each trip, for Ministers, Pastors, and even older teens who are making plans to enter the ministry.

I still complain, just a little, about the harsh conditions I must endure when I go to Haiti. After each trip, Djumy will ask, "when are you coming back?" "Probably not ever," is usually my response. But, given a little time to recuperate, the Lord has a way of letting me know what He wants, even when to go back to Haiti. **It's pretty hard to resist the love shown by the Haitian people every time I go there. That's just one of the blessings of experiencing "Pure Religion."**

WHAT IS SO DIFFERENT IN OUR "INNER CITIES?"

In some ways, it is no different. Inner city children, orphaned, or neglected, need love and care. In other ways, it is very different. Many children in our inner cities have never known their fathers. Over 80 percent of the teens in juvenile court have not had a Dad at home to grow up with. Sadly, most of the moms of inner-city children have been abandoned by the baby's "daddy." **These inner-city children, and their moms, are not exactly in the same category as "third-world" orphans and widows, but there is a very serious need for "looking after them in their 'distress.'"**

"WHAT'S A WHITE GUY LIKE YOU......?"

Sally and I knew that we would be entering a totally different type of ministry when we accepted the Lord's call to establish a ministry, including a church, in the inner city of Memphis. From the very beginning, we found such a tremendous, welcoming response by the families living in Lauderdale Courts, the Public Housing community located near St. Jude Hospital. It was in no time at all that we were considered "family" to the local residents. (Over 2,000 were living in this one Housing Project.) We would find ourselves, many times into the evenings, visiting with the residents in their homes. We met people of all ages: families; children; elderly residents. When Memphis Inner City Church opened its doors in 1990, the people responded very enthusiastically! God was so good to put us exactly where He wanted us. **I guess you could say, "God set us up!"**

He had put such a love in our hearts for these people that we could not resist, or say "no" to His call.

Obviously, our (ongoing) presence in the inner city drew a lot of attention - and a lot of questions. Many had doubts as to our motives. **I was often asked, "what's a white guy like you doing down here in a place like this?" My answer was always the same: "I believe if it were Jesus, this is where He would be, where the most need is."** Everyone seemed to agree. We didn't need to go into detail about what, or who, those needs referred to. It was obvious. Lauderdale Courts, and the other 22 Public Housing projects in Memphis, had become havens for crime, drugs, gangs, violence, and more. At the same time, there were whole families there that had never known anything, or anywhere, else as their homes. We were truly blessed to have become a part of that community.

"GOD, WHAT DO YOU WANT US TO DO WITH ALL THESE KIDS?"

As soon as the church was established, we began programs for the children and teenagers. Sally and I, and Sally's daughter, Ellen, worked together to form several choirs: a children's choir; a middle-school age choir; and a teen choir. Even though this required weekly rehearsals, and weekly performances, by and for each choir, it was well worth it. **The middle and teen choirs even made out of town choir trips to sing in churches throughout the mid-south states. The teen choir, and Sally's adult choir, were responsible for raising over $5,000 for our new building program.** Yes, it was somewhat challenging to do that, but it proved to be very beneficial. It made a profound impact on their lives - and ours also! It was not always easy going. One Wednesday night, when I was out of town on tour, Sally was taking care of the teen choir rehearsal, when two

131

of the boys got into a fight. Rather than call the police, she just jumped in between them and broke it up! They had such respect for her that they obeyed her. Thank God! Just about all of these kids, all ages, were from dysfunctional homes, rarely with a "father" figure to learn from.

WHAT COULD WE DO TO HELP THE CHILDREN - EDUCATIONALLY?

We saw another great need, to help these children with their education. So many would fall behind in school. Many would fail, which would likely lead to criminal behavior, not to mention their futures: family, careers. So, with the help of area churches and community institutions, we began a weekly "tutoring" program. God sent many wonderful volunteers who gladly spent at least one night a week to help these inner city kids. **Although we had many participants, two people really stood out in helping to organize the tutoring program, which would mean helping scores of kids, perhaps nearly 100 each week, with their schooling. Dick and Carolyn Apple, members of the East Win Church, took the lead. Without people like Dick & Carolyn, it would not have been possible**. This amazing couple continues to this day to pray, encourage, and support this mission. Every one of our volunteers were demonstrating "Pure Religion," in the inner city of Memphis.

DID ALL STORIES HAVE HAPPY ENDINGS?

Sadly, we were witnesses to some tragic situations. One of our teens, who had become a national, Junior Golden Gloves Boxing Champion, became involved in drugs. As a result, he lost his title, and was banned from the local gym, just a block from the church. All of his awards, pictures, and posters were removed. His was not a one-time offense, but multiple arrests were involved. **The last time I saw him, he was in line, as a young adult, to get a shelter voucher at the Union Mission. He was homeless.**

Another young man, whose single mother always brought him to church as a child, lost a big part of who he was, and almost lost his life. He was even in the Children's Choir, was baptized into Christ, and rarely missed an activity. However, when he grew to be a teenager, he was no longer faithful or interested in church youth activities. One night his mother called me. She was totally panicked and distraught! "My son was in a serious car wreck. He's still unconscious and in the hospital. And, **they're telling me that, in order to save his life, he must have both legs cut off! I now have to decide what to do!" The next day she informed me that he had lost his legs. She couldn't bear to lose her son.** What happened? What caused the wreck? Drugs. He was driving his car while being pursued by "drug dealers." When he crashed into the back of a parked truck, his car exploded into flames that should have killed him.

A third example: another mom, who was married, had four children, whom she brought to church every Sunday, plus all youth activities. As each child grew older, she would say, "I will soon have another one ready to be baptized." All four came to know Christ as Savior. Her husband, however, would constantly be in and out of jail, on and off drugs and alcohol, robbing his own family of their resources to support his habits. He was very friendly, and religious, when he was sober. **Still, the mother of the children remained steadfast to her faith and raised her children to become educated, and successful in life. She had always worked at a good, steady job in order to support the family. As to the husband / father, he eventually lost his life in a shooting in West Memphis. Thank God for faithful "inner city" moms!**

"ARE YOU AND YOUR WIFE GONNA GET MARRIED?

Wasn't there a little bit of "culture shock" involved in going to the inner city? Yes. We had a lot to learn. One day, as Sally and I pulled into the parking lot of our "warehouse church," **one of our ten-year old girls was there as we got out of the car. She surprised us when she said to me, "are you and your wife gonna get married?" Of course, we were already married. But, in her world, most couples just "live together," even having children, until, at some later date, they might get married, legally. In the meantime, your "partner" is your wife, or husband.** We also learned, the hard way, that many, who become "couples," simply say, "this is my fiancé." What it often means is, "yes, we are living together, and no, we may not ever get married." We refused to allow anyone on staff, or in the choir, to openly live in open disobedience to God's will. As a result, we lost more than one Associate Minister, and one of our lead soloists in the teen choir. We don't believe that anyone was loved less, or not treated with kindness, when these things happened. But we also believe that God will only bless those who are truly His, no matter what their issues may be. As He is forgiving, so must we be as well.

WHAT'S THE REAL LESSON IN 1 CORINTHIANS, CHAPTER 13?

Maybe we have always just been trying to explain what each phrase or verse means. While we found that those in the inner city may not have known the Bible like we did, they did know the difference in real love, and what was not! Being loved and accepted by these people meant so much to us. And we know that they only wanted to know that we truly cared about them. That's what we believe 1 Corinthians should mean: patience; kindness; humility; truthfulness; and love. Yes, the "greatest of these is love." All talents and abilities, gifts of the Spirit, knowledge, and sacrifices, mean nothing compared to love. This should be the loudest message coming to all of us today!

1 Corinthians 13:3-7 (MSG) *"If I give everything I own to the poor and even go to the stake to be burned as a martyr, but I don't love, I've gotten nowhere. So, no matter what I say, what I believe, and what I do, I'm bankrupt without love.*

4 Love never gives up. Love cares more for others than for self. Love doesn't want what it doesn't have. Love doesn't strut, doesn't have a swelled head,

5 Doesn't force itself on others, isn't always "me first," doesn't fly off the handle, doesn't keep score of the sins of others,

6 Doesn't revel when others grovel, takes pleasure in the flowering of truth,

7 Puts up with anything, trusts God always, always looks for the best, never looks back, but keeps going to the end."

ARE WE REALLY "HIS" PEOPLE, KNOWN BY OUR LOVE?

I don't know about you, but I never want to be known as a "phoney," someone who says, "I'll just fake it until I make it."

Dear Lord, Jesus: help me, by Your Holy Spirit within me, to love as you love, especially those who need love the most. In Your Name. Amen

SOMETHING TO THINK ABOUT:

Who do I find hardest to love?

CHAPTER 16

"MAKE DISCIPLES OF ALL THE NATIONS!" REALLY?

Matthew 28:18-20 (NKJV)
And Jesus came and spoke to them, saying, "All authority has been given to Me in heaven and on earth.

19 "Go therefore and make disciples of all the nations, baptizing them in the name of the Father and of the Son and of the Holy Spirit,

20 "teaching them to observe all things that I have commanded you; and lo, I am with you always, even to the end of the age."
Amen.

"BUT, SHANE, THERE'S TOO MANY OF THEM!"

Have you ever felt so "overwhelmed" by a situation that you just "gave up," before you even got started? World evangelism may seem much too daunting, but is that all He is referring to? If we are not reaching the lost in our own vicinity, it's unlikely that we will go around the world to do it. Having a heart for souls works from the inside out. If the Lord is in my heart, He will not stay silent. Neither will I. When I step into the arena, God is right there with me. He always wins!

One of my favorite movies of all time is "Shane," the story of how one man took on the "bad guys," who were making life miserable for early settlers in our country as they migrated west. Little Joey, about 10 years old, watched as Shane, a reforming gun fighter, who was now working for a local "homesteader," wound up in a fistfight in the saloon when they mocked him, and prodded him into fighting back. While he was winning the fight, when it was just one of them, several more jumped in to make sure he was beaten. That's when Joey, the son of the homesteader Shane was working for, came into the saloon and whispered, "Shane, there's too many of them!" Well, if you saw the movie, you know that's when the homesteader decided to help Shane out. The two of them literally "whipped" a whole bunch of the bad guys! **Now, that's my kind of movie! I was about 12 at the time, living in San Francisco. I still relive that scene in the movie to this day.**

WHAT ARE WE SUPPOSED TO DO WHEN THE ODDS ARE AGAINST US?

Shane got the help he needed. So can we. Was Jesus being unrealistic when He commanded his "few" disciples to "tell the whole world "About Him? He even told them to go... *"to the end of the earth!"* *Acts 1:8.* We actually learn very quickly what the first disciples thought about it. Yes, they did evangelize all of Jerusalem, Judea, and Samaria, although Samaria would have to wait awhile. They were more than willing to share Christ in and around where they lived. So, what would it take for them to expand and go into other countries? Nothing less than outright "persecution!" They were being shaken and uprooted, out of their comfortable surroundings. Again, let's don't be too hard on them. Would we have done the same thing? **No one that I know really wants to be forced out of** their "comfort zone." But, in order for the Holy Spirit to re-plant us, He usually has to "uproot" us from where we are.

Acts 8:1-4 (KJV) *"And Saul was consenting unto his death. And at that time there was a great persecution against the church which was at Jerusalem; and they were all scattered abroad throughout the regions of Judaea and Samaria, except the apostles.*

2 And devout men carried Stephen to his burial, and made great lamentation over him.

3 As for Saul, he made havoc of the church, entering into every house, and hauling men and women, and committed them to prison.

4 ¶ Therefore they that were scattered abroad went everywhere preaching the word

DID YOU NOTICE WHO WAS NOW "PREACHING THE WORD"?

"They were all scattered.... except the apostles!" First-time converts were now "Evangelists," spreading the gospel of Christ. As they were being "scattered," they weren't forced to talk about Christ. He was now their reason for living. They were more than ready for the challenge, even though they hadn't even finished burying Stephen yet! They just needed a little "nudging" to get started. Perhaps some of us could use a little "nudging" to get us out there for Jesus?

My experiences have shown me that many Christians (church members) do not see themselves "going into all the world," or even next door. And they are perhaps not being taught, or shown how, to successfully share their faith with the lost. Maybe they see it as being for those willing and able to do those kinds of things." Many church members may never see the "Great Commission" as a personal responsibility, or an opportunity. At one time, there used to be much more emphasis on personal evangelism programs in our local churches, where members would meet at least one night a week, and go out two-by-two, to knock on doors and visit people in their homes, and even set up home Bible studies. Since times have, indeed, changed so much, we must develop new methods for each new generation to replace older, obsolete methods. We need methods that don't keep us locked away so much of the time on our computers, away from real people. Actually, some churches have done so, and are doing it very well. But, have the majority of our churches not been successful in implementing new evangelism methods**? Personal contact is still the most effective way to win people to Christ. How about, if I not only invite someone to church, but, also to lunch after church services?** Or, if new people show up at our church service, why not invite them to lunch, instead of eating alone or going with the same group we always do? If we have such a plan in mind, in advance, it may mean the difference in a lost soul being saved. This is just one way to do "personal evangelism."

In Acts, chapter 8, it wasn't the trained, educated, or experienced ones who went "everywhere, preaching the word." It was the common, ordinary, inexperienced, but excited, believers. It was those who had tasted and knew that "the Lord is good!" That's really the best qualification ever!

"BUT, WHAT IF I'M JUST NOT COMFORTABLE WITH CERTAIN PEOPLE?"

Even more reason to "get out of the box." When we first went into the inner city, we knew God had a special blessing in store for us.

Same thing at the County Jail. How did we know that? He said so. He promised that His Presence, the Holy Spirit, would always be with us.

Deuteronomy 31:8 (MSG) *"GOD is striding ahead of you. He's right there with you. He won't let you down; he won't leave you. Don't be intimidated. Don't worry."*

Even Jesus relied on the Father's promise of His Presence: **John 8:29 (NKJV)** *"And He who sent Me is with Me. The Father has not left Me alone, for I always do those things that please Him."*

We never talked "race" in the Inner-City Church, nor in our personal conversations. Why not? To do so would immediately cause people to take sides, to create division where there would otherwise be none. What we did do was treat everyone the same. **If God is "no respecter of persons," neither should we be. But it must be genuine.** While our membership was predominately African American, there were people from many different races and cultures. I would sometimes say to the church, "I will never be the same color as you, and you will never be the same color as me." So, lets be "one people, the people of God." This is how we bring "glory" to God. God has a way of working out even our most obvious differences, if we give everything over to Him. We actually had many wonderful experiences that were brought about by our "differences." Can we possibly practice "Pure Religion," if we show favoritism?

DOESN'T "POLITICS" SOMETIMES GET IN THE WAY?

There is no doubt that we will have political preferences, and differences, in any church. But are we not called to minister to everyone the same? Yes, there are things we must uphold and practice in our lives, teachings that the Bible clearly defines as right or wrong. However, if someone is determined to promote political views and positions in the church, it may well alienate people who need the Lord. There certainly have been, and still are, "troublemakers," whose goal is to divide others for their own personal agenda. **Memphis is known, perhaps more than anything else, as the City where Dr. Martin Luther King, Jr. was assassinated. There is no place on earth that unity, both racial and spiritual, is needed more than in Memphis.** How is that even possible? Through the church, the Body of Christ. It need not be a political issue. There are laws prohibiting using the church as a political platform, even though some churches openly defy those laws. We never did.

It was a "breath of fresh air" for many local residents to see our ministry teams, made up of different races, working side-by-side. What doesn't work is, for one side to work against others who are in the same fellowship. **True unity is somewhat "miraculous," when you think about it. Our whole society is divided along so many lines, race and culture, it is imperative that the church be "one body," the Body of Christ.**

John 17:20-21 (NIV) *"My prayer is not for them alone. I pray also for those who will believe in me through their message,*

21 that all of them may be one, Father, just as you are in me and I am in you. May they also be in us so that the world may believe that you have sent me."

Ephesians 4:1-6 (NIV) *"As a prisoner for the Lord, then, I urge you to live a life worthy of the calling you have received.*

2 Be completely humble and gentle; be patient, bearing with one another in love.

3 Make every effort to keep the unity of the Spirit through the bond of peace.

4 There is one body and one Spirit—just as you were called to one hope when you were called—

5 one Lord, one faith, one baptism;

6 one God and Father of all, who is over all and through all and in all."

I am convinced that most of us truly believe in, and want, unity in the body of Christ. The problem is, many may not be willing to do what it takes to accomplish this unity. It requires determination and perseverance, rather than to accept something less. It doesn't mean that we must give up our own traditions and worship preferences for the sake of unity. Rather, it means that we actually "seek out" opportunities to worship and work alongside people who are different from us. We can certainly learn much from them. And we may find ourselves truly enjoying their fellowship.

SHOULDN'T WE AVOID CHURCHES WE DON'T AGREE WITH?

I have to admit that I was raised to look at all other churches with a suspicious eye. Why? Because they couldn't be trusted. While I do believe that our leaders always had our best interest in mind, primarily where doctrine was concerned, it seemed unfortunate that we were more like adversaries, rather than part of the same body of Christ. **So, to this day, we still see this mistrust of every denominational group that is not of our fellowship. We even call ourselves, "non-denominational." There's nothing wrong with that, unless it makes us feel "superior" to others.** If we are, in fact, more correct, doctrinally, shouldn't this make us more "humble?"

More loving? Not "holier-than-thou." I shudder to think what the Lord thinks of me when I see myself as better than "those other people."

As I have said earlier, "my working with other church groups doesn't mean that my beliefs have changed." It does, however, mean that I have a responsibility to be true to my core beliefs, while at the same time being a blessing to others, and to be humble enough to work alongside some with whom I disagree. Some may even say that I have "denied the faith," or, "compromised my beliefs." If I am afraid of criticism, of what some of my friends or acquaintances may say, or think, then I am letting them dictate who I am. I don't think so. I have seen too much arrogance and judgmentalism where there should be humility instead**. Something else I have learned as I have worked with other churches, just about every other denomination feels exactly as we do, that they are right and we are wrong!**

DO I FIND IT HARD TO "HUMBLE" MYSELF?

I became good friends with a man, now deceased, whom I considered a giant for God, with many accomplishments to confirm it: books; seminars; and a charming personality. His name: **Carl Ketcherside.** He was always in great demand as a speaker. Carl's church background was much the same as mine, very strict doctrinally. However, in his later years, he found fellowship with churches other than his own. I heard him once say, "If you pinch a Methodist you get the same response as any one of us." He was just saying, "Let's acknowledge our human likenesses, then get on with the business of doing the Lord's work." That didn't make him a Methodist, but it caused many people to want to hear what he had to say**. I don't know a lot of other details of his final years, except that he had** established a mission to the inner city of Saint Louis, ministering to the homeless and the poor, which included a church. To me, that says it all. What really matters to God is what also matters to people: do you love me enough to show it?

Luke 14:11 (NKJV) *"For whoever exalts himself will be humbled, and he who humbles himself will be exalted."*

James 4:6 (NKJV) *But He gives more grace. Therefore, He says: "God resists the proud, But gives grace to the humble."*

Luke 18:9-14 Also *He spoke this parable to some who trusted in themselves that they were righteous, and despised others:*

10 "Two men went up to the temple to pray, one a Pharisee and the other a tax collector.

11 "The Pharisee stood and prayed thus with himself, 'God, I thank You that I am not like other men—extortioners, unjust, adulterers, or even as this tax collector.

12 'I fast twice a week; I give tithes of all that I possess.'

13 "And the tax collector, standing afar off, would not so much as raise his eyes to heaven, but beat his breast, saying, 'God, be merciful to me a sinner!'

14 "I tell you, this man went down to his house justified rather than the other; for everyone who exalts himself will be humbled, and he who humbles himself will be exalted."

HAVE I BEEN "DISOBEYING" THE GREAT COMMISSION?

Where and when have I drawn the line as to who I will, or will not, take the gospel of Christ? I don't see Jesus making exceptions in the

Great Commission (Matthew 28:18-20), like we sometimes do. Much like Jonah, sometimes we justify our actions, or inactions, with our own reasons for not going "into all the world," or, to "those people" who may even live not that far from us. Shouldn't I be praying for the body of Christ - around the world? Isn't the Holy Spirit waiting for me to get in step with Him, so that He can lead me to opportunities which are already there, no matter where "there" is? Doesn't every church have a responsibility to honestly try and reach everyone, regardless of background, who lives in the neighborhood where our church is located? **While it is true that people of different cultures and races may prefer their own churches and styles of worship, which is understandable, should we not let them know they are welcome to worship and work with us? If so, our invitations must be genuine.**

ARE "SHORT-TERM" MISSION TRIPS OF ANY REAL VALUE?

A "short-term" mission trip suggests a time period of perhaps 10 days to several weeks. This has become very popular in recent decades. In earlier times, almost all "foreign" missionaries would plan to be away for years, and some perhaps for the rest of their lives. I am just a part-timer to short-term mission trips, having made over 30 such trips in the past 15 years. These trips have literally changed my whole life! I praise God for the many, many blessings I have experienced as a result of these trips.

Finally, let me tell you about another very remarkable man, **Buford Garrett**, a Christian Minister, also now deceased, whom I met in his later years. He had just returned from a short-term mission trip to Mexico. He was overwhelmed with what he had experienced on that, his first mission trip. He was very emotional each time he talked about it. **While serving others, the very poor and disadvantaged, in Mexico, his relationship with the Lord, and his faith, deepened far more than he had ever known before.**

Soon after his return from Mexico, Buford came to visit our Memphis Inner City Church. He was amazed at the opportunities he saw to be a part of something similar to his experiences in Mexico, helping the very poor, but now through a local ministry, much closer to his home. He soon began driving every Sunday from his home in Mississippi, a distance of about an hour each way. Since he was a retired minister, with years of service, he began to participate in our services. Sometimes he would preach or teach. He joined the adult choir, and was eventually added to our Board of Directors. **He had added a true sense of "love and compassion" to our work here. Would that have happened if not for his "short-term" mission trip to Mexico?** What we do know, for sure, is that he already had a heart devoted to God. "Pure Religion" was already his goal and purpose in life.

Precious Lord, please use me to let others know just how "precious" You really are, by showing unconditional love and acceptance of whoever they are. As You have been to me, may I be to them. I believe that is the meaning of "Pure Religion." In Jesus' name. Amen

SOMETHING TO THINK ABOUT:

What do I think is the best way to evangelize the world?

CHAPTER 17

DO LEADERS BEAR GREATER RESPONSIBILITY?

Luke 6:39 (NLT)
Then Jesus gave the following illustration: "What good is it for one blind person to lead another? The first one will fall into a ditch and pull the other down also."

WHAT SHOULD WE DO WHEN WE FAIL - BADLY?

I called home to give Sally an update on my trip to North Carolina. I asked, "how are things going at the Inner-City Church?" "I'll tell you when you get back home," she said. I immediately knew it must be pretty bad, just by the way she said it. So, she went ahead and told me.

We were several years into this new church. And, since we were growing, we now had hired two associate ministers. Each one had a church van, used for picking up people for church activities, and for deliveries. Then, we thought it would be a good idea if we rented a two-bedroom apartment where they could both stay, saving us a little money. They usually got along well together, until one of them (the more aggressive one) began "taunting" the other, more passive, one. That's when the weaker one had all he could take. He picked up the glass lamp in their living room and slammed the other one in the face, breaking his nose. The ruckus was by now being heard by others in adjoining apartments. Both the police and an ambulance were called as it was by now a neighborhood event! **When the medics and officers arrived, one of them asked, "Is it true you both work for the Memphis Inner City Church?" They answered, proudly, "yes, we do!" By now the news media had gotten wind of it, making it "unwanted" publicity for our ministry!**

When I arrived home from my trip, I went to V. A. Hospital to see the one who got the short end of the deal. Not only was his nose broken, but his left eye was also bruised and closed! He admitted that he had miscalculated, and misread, what the reaction of the other associate minister would be, in response to his taunting him. I believe he apologized to the other one for what he had done, and vowed to never do anything like that again! Confession and repentance are both "good for the soul." While neither of them was fired, some serious changes and improvements were in order. **Our mission was not just saving souls and helping the poor, it also meant that we had to mentor and train our inexperienced, associate ministers. Even though both of them had already been to Bible College, they hadn't yet learned how to work together.**

ISN'T THERE A SHORTAGE OF "QUALIFIED" LEADERS IN OUR CHURCHES?

It's not just in the church. Just take a look around and we will see a lack of strong leaders who are men and women of integrity in just about every category, including business and politics. Do a lot of churches select leaders who are not ready nor qualified, just to fill an open position, or to appease somebody for favors? A leadership position in our Lord's church is nothing to take lightly, especially when it involves being responsible for everything from the children programs, reaching the lost, and to "shepherding the flock," as elders. **People may want to be leaders for the wrong reasons, such as power, personal influence, and control. This usually leads to abuse and neglect of the parishioners.** In more serious circumstances, it may also lead to division in the church as a result of "power struggles."

DOESN'T IT REALLY COME DOWN TO "CHARACTER?"

I have had opportunities to conduct Leadership Conferences in several countries, and in most cases, it will be for several days at the same location, and will involve at least a hundred or more church leaders. It is always a very special time for me and, I believe, for those who are attending also. In most locations, because of such a need, it could easily be an annual event, with a full house every time. I am not sure that my lessons would fit in most churches here in the U. S. Why? Because we focus primarily on the "Characteristics of Servant Leaders." This has to do with integrity, motive, dedication, and desire. What's in the heart of the true leader?

I don't deal so much with methods of church growth, techniques, or whether someone meets the "qualifications" of a leader, as in the local church by-laws. (Spiritual, Biblical qualifications are always a "must!") **How many times have we chosen leaders for very important responsibilities based solely on their availability and their agreement to fill a position?**

ISN'T IT RIGHT THERE TO SEE, IF WE LOOK FOR IT?

If we take each chapter of the book of Acts, beginning with chapter one, what were the characteristics of the leaders? And what should they look for in future leaders? When Judas, the apostle who betrayed Jesus and hung himself, needed to be replaced, why did they choose Matthias, instead of Barsabas? Both had met the qualifications, but they could only choose one. Then they prayed,

24 "Lord, you know everyone's heart. Show us which of these two you have chosen

25 to take over this apostolic ministry, which Judas left to go where he belongs."

26 Then they cast lots, and the lot fell to Matthias; so he was added to the eleven apostles. **Acts 1:24-26 (NIV)** God caused Matthias to be chosen because He knew his heart. Matthias had "humility," one of the essential characteristics of a "great, servant leader!"

<u>**Once we have those who are qualified, according to our technical rules, we must pray for God's wisdom as to whom He chooses. If we ask, He will tell us.**</u> Other characteristics that we see in the early church leaders in Acts include Unity - able and willing to work together; obedience; Holy Spirit filled; courage; boldness; willing to speak out; helping others; giving glory to God; rejoicing in Him; unashamed; unafraid; prayerful: and, on and on. These are personal qualities, the kind of things we don't usually talk about when selecting leaders. But, shouldn't we be more careful, and prayerfully put it totally in God's hands? <u>**Even when we choose the right ones, the ones God chooses, they will still face enormous challenges every day. They might even disagree, or not get along with co-ministers. The Holy Spirit will always give us guidance, if we ask.**</u>

WHY ARE SO MANY YOUNG, EDUCATED LEADERS DROPPING OUT?

The dropout rate among young ministers is known to be very high. Perhaps over 90 percent, even youth ministers, will leave the ministry in just a few years. Why is that? There are a lot of reasons, including unmet expectations and discouragement. In many cases, the young minister perhaps has been educated in almost everything, except how to relate to people, or what to do when pressures and responsibilities are too heavy to bear. **Have they learned the importance of daily, spiritual growth in the Lord which involves a deepening, daily prayer and personal worship walk with God? Is Jesus the closest and dearest friend one could ever have?**

DON'T WE NEED ROLE MODELS AND MENTORS?

Are there those we can look up to go to, or talk to, who understands what we are going through? Would it not be a good idea to meet with someone on a regular basis whose company would be an encouragement to us, even if it was just for coffee. I thank God for role models that were both inspiring and challenging to me. Just look at the relationship between the apostle Paul and young Timothy. **Timothy became a "strong" leader because Paul took such an interest in him and helped him in many, very important ways. We all need someone in our lives like that. If you can't think of someone, pray about it. God knows.**

2 Timothy 2:1-3 (NKJV) *"You therefore, my son, be strong in the grace that is in Christ Jesus.*

2 And the things that you have heard from me among many witnesses, commit these to faithful men who will be able to teach others also.

3 You therefore must endure hardship as a good soldier of Jesus Christ."

Paul, the apostle, who used to be called Saul, was such a strong influence on Timothy because he had been "obedient" to the Lord's call on his life. Compare him to Saul, the first king of Israel, who was a miserable failure, and a disgrace to the people of God in the Old Testament. Why? Because he was not obedient. Plus, he thought only of himself. His life, and kingship, ended in miserable failure. Even his own son, Jonathan, rejected him in favor of friendship with David, the shepherd boy who became king after Saul. Because king Saul disobeyed God, God rejected Saul as king. **So, make sure your role models and mentors are people of character before God.**

1 Samuel 15:23-26 (NIV) *"For rebellion is like the sin of divination, and arrogance like the evil of idolatry. Because you have rejected the word of the LORD, he has rejected you as king."*

24 Then Saul said to Samuel, "I have sinned. I violated the LORD's command and your instructions. I was afraid of the people and so I gave in to them.

25 Now I beg you, forgive my sin and come back with me, so that I may worship the LORD."

26 But Samuel said to him, "I will not go back with you. You have rejected the word of the LORD, and the LORD has rejected you as king over Israel!"

HOW IMPORTANT IS A LEADER'S PERSONALITY?

Well, it's a lot better to be "liked," than to be "disliked!" But it's a known fact, we all can learn how to be better persons, to improve our personality. When I was in my early 20's, I realized that I was not doing very well with my people skills, especially as a young minister. So, I went out and bought Dale Carnegie's book, "How to Win Friends and Influence People," now published by **General Press, New Delhi, India.** I literally "devoured" that book! I think it helped me a lot. I might even read it again. Wouldn't hurt!

While we all have a "personality," we also have our "individuality." Or individuality is our "self," which tends to become our way of "getting our way." **Oswald Chambers** writes about this in **"My Utmost For His Highest,"** "Individuality is the husk of the personal life. Individuality is all elbows; it separates and isolates. Individuality must go in order that the personal life may come out and be brought into fellowship with God."

I believe this is what Jesus was referring to when he said:

23 "If any of you wants to be my follower, you must put aside your selfish ambition, shoulder your cross daily, and follow me.

24 If you try to keep your life for yourself, you will lose it. But if you give up your life for me, you will find true life. **Luke 9:23-24 (NLT)**

An old hymn says it well: "All to Jesus I surrender; all to Him I freely give."

THE STORY OF ONE "REMARKABLE" WOMAN!

Roy and Bonnie Walters have teamed up with me on two of my mission trips to China. Both Roy and Bonnie are very "mission minded." Both have retired and are leading the "WEE CELEBRATE CLASS, young children, at New Hope Christian Church in Bartlett, TN, also my home church. Roy is also Chairman of the New Hope Missions program. They have been a blessing on these trips to China as we worked in some very interesting situations, with very interesting people. One such person is **Nancy, a wonderful Chinese Christian lady**. (Nancy is her U. S. name) Nancy has invited us into her home, and into many churches in China, ranging from thousands of members to house churches. Nancy is a great leader, respected by every church in China where they are acquainted with her. I believe she can talk her way into any church in China (and there are thousands), as she has such a God-given talent (gift) for talking to anyone, including strangers. **There are churches in China that have started as a result of Nancy talking to someone on the street, or in a restaurant, about Jesus!** There are just too many stories to tell involving Nancy and her witnessing for the Lord. She doesn't consider herself a "Preacher," just someone who loves the Lord, and loves to talk about Him.

"MASSAGE PARLOR" EVANGELISM?

Here's just one Nancy story: On our most recent trip to China, Nancy had us scheduled at a house church one of the evenings. She said, "One of their church members has a "Massage Parlor," right on the way. She is offering us a "free" massage, if we want it, on our way to church. After we thought about it, for a few seconds, we said, "why not?" **We really didn't know what we were getting into, but we trusted Nancy. If she says, "it's all right," then it's all right.**

When we arrived at the Parlor, we soon learned that this was not a house of "ill-repute," but a very professional massage parlor, that anyone could go to. It was also a training center for people learning the profession. The massage was great, more so for some of us than others. Before we left, **Nancy was already sharing Christ with everyone, including other guests. She was handing out Bibles and Christian literature to everyone. So, yes, it was in fact "Massage Parlor" evangelism! I think we need a few more Nancy's in the world!**

ISN'T THIS A JOB FOR THE HOLY SPIRIT?

When it's all said and done, I believe we need a lot more "Spirit-filled" Christians who are "on fire" for the Lord. ("Spirit-filled" is not code for charismatic, rather; someone "filled" with Jesus.) Didn't Jesus talk to people everywhere He went? The Holy Spirit, in us, is always looking for someone to talk to about Jesus. And, when He leads into these situations, we surely don't want to ignore what He is wanting to do through us. Everyone knows how difficult it is, sometimes, to talk about Jesus. **We might just need to go see Nancy, and see how the Holy Spirit is working in and through her to reach people for Christ. She has even been referred to by some as, "the apostle Paul of China."**

We, the church, desperately need leaders, now more than ever. We need leaders with character and integrity. That's what this chapter is all about. Can we pray for the Holy Spirit to show us how to raise up these kinds of leaders?

Dear God, help us, while there is still time, to train men and women to be great leaders in our churches, men and women who know the true meaning of "Pure Religion!" In Jesus' Name. Amen

SOMETHING TO THINK ABOUT:

What, and who, makes a great leader?

CHAPTER 18

IS FERVENT PRAYER THAT IMPORTANT?

James 5:16 (NKJV)
"Confess your trespasses to one another, and pray for one another, that you may be healed. The effective, fervent prayer of a righteous man avails much."

James 5:16 (MSG)
"Make this your common practice: Confess your sins to each other and pray for each other so that you can live together whole and healed. The prayer of a person living right with God is something powerful to be reckoned with."

HAVE YOU EVER PRAYED SO HARD YOU BEGAN TO SWEAT?

I sometimes visited one particular elderly resident living in the Barry Homes high rise across the street from our warehouse church. Although she did not attend our church on a regular basis, she was truly a joy to be with. One day she told me, "I pray for you often. And, if you have any special needs, please let me know." Then, what she said next really surprised me. **"When it"s something very important to me, I will kneel and pray until I'm drenched with**

<u>**sweat! That's what I will do for you.**</u> It's no wonder God blessed us so many times in this inner-city mission. I know of a lot more people, in many states, who were also continually praying for us.

"WHY CAN'T I PRAY LIKE MILDRED!"

One of our best members at Memphis Inner City Church was Arthur. Arthur walked slowly, with a limp. Years earlier he had been shot, by a gun, in the hip. The bullet was never removed. Arthur always came to church early and left late. He volunteered for anything needing to be done<u>. **One day after morning worship services he said to me, "Someday I hope I can pray like Mildred."**</u> Mildred, a Christian businesswoman, started coming to our fellowship when a friend invited her. This friend was riding the city bus when it stopped in front of our building while we were singing worship songs. She came, then invited her friend, Mildred. Mildred kept coming because, as she put it, "I loved the music, the worship." Mildred would sometimes pray openly during the services. Her voice was loud and passionate! It was a blessing to hear Mildred pray.

When Arthur heard Mildred pray, he knew he wanted to pray just like her. The only problem with that was, Arthur was very quiet and laid back. Yes, he also liked to pray publicly. But now he felt that he was missing something, that maybe he wasn't as spiritual as he should be. I felt for him. So I told Arthur, <u>**"You will never be able to pray like Mildred. And, God doesn't want you to. God wants you to be who you are. God hears all of us just the same." He agreed, somewhat. I know he still wanted to pray like Mildred.**</u>

WHEN SAM PRAYED, EVEN GOD LISTENED!

I was just a boy when I first heard **Sam Haman** pray in church. He was a bachelor and lived alone. I think he usually walked several miles to church, when he came. Our minister would often call on Sam to say the prayer during services. There would be a "stillness" throughout the building when he began to pray. With a quivering voice, he raised his right hand toward heaven, then began to pray. I was always emotionally moved, even as a boy, when he began to talk to God. It was like no one else was in the room. **He was not loud, nor long-winded. He spoke from the heart, like only God really knew what was in his heart, perhaps hurts none of the rest of us knew about.**

DO WE NEED MORE PRAYER WARRIORS AS MENTORS?

I was in High School when I first heard **Don DeWelt** preach at the Kiamichi Christian Men's Clinic, attended each year by thousands at one time. It was located just 20 miles from where I grew up in Southeast Oklahoma. I was so moved and impressed by his passion and skill as a preacher. He was also a college professor and an author of many books. When I enrolled in Ozark Bible College, I was privileged to take several classes under his teaching. Throughout the years to come, Don DeWelt continued to be one of my heros in the faith.

When we invited Don DeWelt to be a featured speaker at one of our **"Servanthood Seminars,"** in Memphis, he stayed with us in our home in midtown Memphis. It was quite an honor for both Sally and me. Before bedtime he said, "Now, I get up about 3:30 in the morning for my personal time with the Lord. I read God's Word, pray, worship, and sometimes sing a song. Where is the best place (room or corner) for me to do that?" We already knew that this was his habit. So, we were both kind of expecting it. It was obvious that this was his secret to a strong and powerful ministry. He wrote many

158

books, including college textbooks, that are still used widely today. **Was he an effective mentor to me? Absolutely! My goal is not to be like Don DeWelt, but to allow God to use me just as He did him.**

DOES PASSIONATE PRAYER ALWAYS LEAD TO PURE RELIGION?

Not necessarily. However, I doubt that anyone ever does much out of the ordinary, except as a result of intense, passionate, prayer to God. I think that in most cases it is a result of *being tired of just being ordinary,* not seeing God working in your life. **I really believe God is looking for people who are totally committed to Him, people who are ready to be used of God. Such people won't be silent, nor will God ignore their requests.** You will keep praying until God says "yes, I will use you." This may take several years, but it will happen. There has been more than one such time in my own life when I asked the Lord, "Is there not a cause?" "Is this all there all there is?" I love it when I know God is speaking to me and I am responding.

2 Chronicles 16:9 (NKJV) *"For the eyes of the LORD run to and fro throughout the whole earth, to show Himself strong on behalf of those whose heart is loyal to Him."*

HOW IMPORTANT WAS PRAYER TO MOSES?

Did Moses miscalculate the cost of discipleship, and the sacrifices he would have to make, when he said "yes" to God's call on his life? Even Moses had to trust God and step out on faith before God could really use him. **It seemed that Moses was always praying, even testing God's reliability, as he led the Israelites out of Egyptian bondage.** There was the wilderness; then, everyone's whining and

159

complaining. Moses reminded God about his own weaknesses. He brought everything to God! When we follow their entire journey to the Promised Land, it is a constant conversation between Moses and God. Because Moses was totally surrendered to God and zealous for God, God honored His promise to be with Moses and give him success in everything he was asked to do**. Moses was not afraid to remind God of His promises. At times, Moses even argued with God, and on occasions changed His mind.**

In reference to this subject, a few months back I made a note to myself which says, "stop groveling and start arguing!" If God gets the idea that we really don't care that much about how something's going to work out, even something life threatening, why should He bother with us? Why should He invest in us? That doesn't mean that He does not love us; it just means that He isn't going to force us to do what He wants**. He wants us to be "willing partners" with Him in His great enterprise on earth. That's what I want. How about you?**

DOES GOD EXPECT US TO BE BOLD TOWARD HIM?

How many times have we prayed passive prayers, not expecting God to really do anything much, especially through us? Wouldn't God prefer that we be bold instead, letting God know that we are dead serious about doing something great for Him? Do you want to go to a foreign country? Or find something closer to home where you can really make a difference? Is there something in particular you have always wanted to do, unselfishly, to make your life count for Jesus? If the answer is "yes," then tell Him. Keep telling Him! If God wants you somewhere else, doing something different than you had ever imagined, **tell Him you are ready for whatever He wants you to do. After all, as a Christian, you and I belong to Him totally**.

160

HOW SHOULD I PRAY BEFORE MAKING IMPORTANT DECISIONS?

If we are talking about venturing out into the vast area of meeting people's needs, including people in other countries, intense prayer is critical. I have many times had someone come up to me and say, "Oh, I would love to go China with you, or Africa, or Cuba." My immediate (inner) reaction is, "No, you probably wouldn't." A lot of people may think of foreign missions as some kind of pleasure trip. While it can be a very enjoyable experience, even exciting, it might require some extreme sacrifices, things that many people would not want do. **What if there is no indoor toilet, or running water for a shower. What if there are 15-hour days of both rough traveling and very demanding activities that you can't avoid? What about extremely long airline flights that you are not prepared for**? However, if someone is clearly led of God to go on a mission trip, He will equip you with everything you need for the task ahead, physically, mentally, and spiritually. For those who are meant for such service, the response of the people wherever you go more than makes up for any sacrifices you may have made. And, as soon as you get back home, you will probably sign up to go again!

AREN'T PASSIONATE PRAYERS SOMETIMES SELFISH?

Absolutely! Here's one example: When we returned from San Francisco to our old home place in Oklahoma I was fourteen years old. Any fourteen-year-old boy living in the Oklahoma hills, needs a horse. We had none and couldn't afford to buy one. All my friends at school had horses and talked about it all the time. One day at school someone said to me, **"There's a man just up the road from the school who has a young horse, maybe two years old, that**

needs to be ridden. He would probably let you take the horse home with you one day after school.

Well, the man did agree to let me take his horse home with me. I led the horse to my home, built a small corral for him, fed him, and began to plan when I might actually ride him. He was very "skiddish," meaning, he didn't want anyone riding him. So, when the time came, I put our old saddle on him, and prepared to mount him. That's when he bolted and ran away. Truth is, I was a little too timid, having lived the "city life" in San Francisco and was just a little afraid of the horse. **So, he took off running through our field, mocking me every time I got close to him. This wasn't even my horse! If I couldn't catch him, let alone ride him, how would I even get him back to his owner?**

So, I prayed, then prayed harder! I really needed a miracle. This horse wasn't going to let me catch him. Then I noticed him standing among some trees, not moving. As I got closer, I noticed that the rope I had put on him got caught around the roots of a tree. He was caught! Praise the Lord! God had pity on me and answered my prayer. The sad thing is I never got to ride the horse. Oh, one more thing, daddy saw the whole thing! I don't want to put in writing

what he had to say about the whole incident. **Haven't we all prayed "fervent" prayers that were selfish, just so we wouldn't look bad?**

(BTW - I love horses. Sally and I have had several riding horses in recent years, but not now.)

IS IT WRONG TO PRAY FOR COMPASSION, IF I DON'T REALLY WANT IT?

I should pray for compassion, precisely because I don't want it! "Lord, please give me a heart of compassion for the poor, the lost, and the oppressed!" On my own I will seldom attempt to reach out to those most in need, including those who are lost and need Christ as Savior. The Bible is filled with admonitions to show love and compassion. The Holy Spirit then brings this to our attention, and it is He Who puts in our hearts the desire to show Christ's love to others. **Sometimes we may not care that much about such people, that is, until something happens to us that touches our hearts. Then, the Lord will make us aware of the needs of others. But, it's up to you and me to respond.** He will not make us do anything. But the Lord will give us opportunities to be a blessing to others just about every day. If we choose to see ourselves as "Jesus," in the flesh (which is what He wants), this takes the focus off ourselves and puts the spotlight on Jesus. Would He ignore the helpless? I don't think so. But, left to myself, I probably will.

The following scripture passages will either inspire us or discourage us, depending on how serious we are about being used to bring glory to God, by helping "the least of these."

Matthew 9:35-36 (NKJV) *"Then Jesus went about all the cities and villages, teaching in their synagogues, preaching the gospel of the kingdom, and healing every sickness and every disease among the people.*

36 But when He saw the multitudes, He was moved with compassion for them, because they were weary and scattered, like sheep having no shepherd."

Matthew 10:42 (NIV) *"And if anyone gives even a cup of cold water to one of these little ones because he is my disciple, I tell you the truth, he will certainly not lose his reward."*

Matthew 25:37-40 *"Then the righteous will answer Him, saying, 'Lord, when did we see You hungry and feed You, or thirsty and give You drink?*

38 'When did we see You a stranger and take You in, or naked and clothe You?

39 'Or when did we see You sick, or in prison, and come to You?'

40 "And the King will answer and say to them, 'Assuredly, I say to you, inasmuch as you did it to one of the least of these My brethren, you did it to Me.'"

WHAT IF I JUST DON'T FEEL LIKE GOING SOMEWHERE TO HELP SOMEONE?

I think all of us feel that way sometimes. I don't know how many times I didn't <u>want</u> to do something for someone else, but when I went ahead and did it, I felt great! Most times after I have gone to the homeless shelter, or to a prison, and shared the love of Christ with them, I almost feel "guilty" for feeling so great! What did I do? It's the Lord they needed, and only the

Lord Who could meet their needs. **<u>Still, I'm the one who is being blessed, and only because I was obedient to the Lord, not because I was anything special in myself.</u>**

When I return from every foreign mission trip, I am so "pumped," so thankful that I made the trip, even though at some point I might have wished that I didn't have to go, and maybe looked for an excuse not to go. However, I always have so many stories to tell about when I get home. I will have met some of the most incredible people on these trips. I have seen the hand of God at work in so many people's lives. **I become an eyewitness to the grace and goodness of God in so many situations. I see people praising the Lord, even when they have so little of this world's goods to call their own. In some cases, they have lost everything due to earthquakes, floods, or hurricanes.** For me, I believe God's promise: "If you do what I ask you to do, there will be special blessings in store for you. And I can tell you, it becomes addictive!

Holy Spirit, make me a vessel that brings glory to God, the Father, by putting me in the vicinity of someone, each day, whom You want to bless through me. In Jesus' name. Amen

SOMETHING TO THINK ABOUT:

Am I satisfied and happy with my prayer life?

CHAPTER 19

WHAT IS THE ESSENCE OF PURE RELIGION?

Luke 5:11b (NKJV)
".... they forsook all and followed Him."

Acts 4:32 (NIV)
"All the believers were one in heart and mind. No-one claimed that any of his possessions was his own, but they shared everything they had."

James 1:27 (NKJV)
Pure and undefiled religion before God and the Father is this: to visit orphans and widows in their trouble, and to keep oneself unspotted from the world.

"SOLD OUT" FOR GOD?

It's kind-of like, you know Pure Religion when you see it. That rare, special person whom everybody wishes they could be. Most churches have at least one. The one who is always ready and willing to do what he or she can to help others. Maybe the one who goes downtown after church services to hand out sandwiches to the homeless. Could be the one who always makes sure that, when a stranger walks in the building, they are greeted and welcomed, especially if they look like they don't fit in.

It's also the one who is truly "sold out" for God. Someone who never thinks about self, but always talks about, praises, and builds up others. It's hard to fake being that person, no matter how hard we want to be that kind of person. I believe it is actually the result of striving every day to get closer to God, and to be just like Jesus in every way. When we study and look deeper into God's Word the kind of life Jesus lived, we come away awed and inspired. And when we examine the work of the Holy Spirit, we see that those in the Bible were empowered to do things, including helping those in need, because they were truly connected to the power source, God Himself! That's why I feel the need to begin every day with the prayer, "Lord, may Your Holy Spirit work in and through me to be a blessing to someone today, and to bear "much fruit" in your kingdom." **When I do this, God, the Father is glorified, Jesus' name is exalted, and I am so much happier than when it's just me, being me.**

AM I LIKE BILL?

Perhaps you've heard the story, "Just Like Bill" (don't know how true it is, but it's great!). It seems that a homeless drifter, Bill, wandered into the local homeless shelter, just as they were meeting for chapel services. He was so powerfully influenced by the speaker's message that he marched forward to kneel and confess his sins before God, and everyone else. Following his conversion, he so wanted to serve Jesus that he volunteered for every dirty job that needed to be done around the mission, for example, like cleaning the toilets. He truly impressed everyone with his servant attitude.

Soon, another homeless man began to notice how devoted Bill was, that he also surrendered to the Lord at invitation time. As he was kneeling at the altar, the mission pastor knelt beside him and heard him say, **"I want to be just like Bill!" That's when the pastor tried to correct him, saying, "don't you mean, you want to be just like Jesus?" The man looked up and said, "Is he like Bill?"**

HOW MUCH IS IT GOING TO COST ME?

Everything! Remember the story of the "Rich Young Ruler," who, though being rich and powerful, lost everything? Why? By making the wrong choice when Jesus told him he must "sell everything he had and give it to the poor."

Mark 10:21-22 (NKJV) *Then Jesus, looking at him, loved him, and said to him, "One thing you lack: Go your way, sell whatever you have and give to the poor, and you will have treasure in heaven; and come, take up the cross, and follow Me."*

22 But he was sad at this word, and went away sorrowful, for he had great possessions.

Not only did he not take any of his riches with him when he died, he also lost the riches of heaven, and, most importantly, eternal life. **Although we may not be rich like he was, we can still have the same sin problem that he had, love for the things of this world.**

JUST WHAT IS IT GOD REALLY WANTS?

Me: All of me. One of the most inspiring accounts of sacrificial giving in the Bible is where Paul wrote about the, very poor, believers of the churches in Macedonia. Macedonia was an ancient kingdom located within the Grecian empire, and had been conquered by Alexander the Great. The Macedonian Christians, though living in extreme poverty, responded to the needs of the Judean believers, as presented to them by Paul. This tells the rest of us that God can use anyone He chooses, regardless of how much, or how little, we have.

2 Corinthians 8:1-5 *"And now, brothers, we want you to know about the grace that God has given the Macedonian churches.*

2 Out of the most severe trial, their overflowing joy and their extreme poverty welled up in rich generosity.

3 For I testify that they gave as much as they were able, and even beyond their ability. Entirely on their own,

4 they urgently pleaded with us for the privilege of sharing in this service to the saints.

5 And they did not do as we expected, but they gave themselves first to the Lord and then to us in keeping with God's will."

WHAT ABOUT MY FAMILY?

Some of the hardest things Jesus asks us to do will involve our families. While there are some very difficult challenges ministers and missionaries must face, God never intended any of us to use our families as an excuse, either to leave them, or to not follow the Lord's call to ministry when family members must be involved or at least be supportive. Sometimes we may have poor judgement when choosing our mates, particularly when both will have to bear the responsibilities associated with ministry obligations. As I have said earlier, **"pray first about everything." When Jesus said we must "hate" father and mother, we believe He is saying, "choose."** When His commandments sometimes seem impossible, He promises to always be right there with us.

Luke 14:25-27 *Large crowds were travelling with Jesus, and turning to them he said:*

26 "If anyone comes to me and does not hate his father and mother, his wife and children, his brothers and sisters—yes, even his own life—he cannot be my disciple.

27 And anyone who does not carry his cross and follow me cannot be my disciple.

Lk 18:28-30 (NIV) *Peter said to him, "We have left all we had to follow you!"*

29 "I tell you the truth," Jesus said to them, "no-one who has left home or wife or brothers or parents or children for the sake of the kingdom of God

30 will fail to receive many times as much in this age and, in the age to come, eternal life."

WHO ARE THEY? CAN WE BE MORE SPECIFIC?

Just who are all these "needy" people? **James, chapter 1**, mentions only two categories: *orphans and widows.* However, several other Bible passages give us a much broader picture of who these people are by identifying them: **Isaiah, chapter 58:** *those in bonds; burdened; oppressed; hungry; poor; naked.* **Luke, chapter 4:** *poor; brokenhearted; captive; blind; oppressed.* **Matthew, chapter 25:** *hungry; thirsty; a stranger; naked; sick; in prison.*

The bottom line is this: Jesus was always for the underdog. That did not mean he supported lawbreakers or lazy people. But He defended those who were being taken advantage of. Today we have a huge problem with people abusing and disrespecting the elderly. **Millions of children are being used as "sex slaves," so their owners can**

get rich. It doesn't take a genius to figure out what God does not approve of.

HOW MUCH AM I OBLIGATED TO USE MY TIME AND MY RESOURCES?

That is a fair question. I believe God just wants us to have a compassionate, servant's heart. So what if we are taken advantage of from time to time. That shouldn't cause us to quit. It should, however, make us wiser. If Jesus had taken that attitude, He would never have made it to the cross! **The more we give, the more will come back to us. While no likes to be used or lied to, real people with real needs, and hurts, will still be there.**

Even Jesus' closest disciples argued with Him about spending too much time with what we would call, "losers." Before He left this earth, Jesus had to actually demonstrate what He was talking about. It was a very hard lesson for them then. It's still one of the hardest lessons we will ever learn today. Only when we learn true humility will we be free to serve others. All we are and all we have belongs to God. He asks us to use what we have wisely.

John 13:2-9 (NLT) *It was time for supper, and the Devil had already enticed Judas, son of Simon Iscariot, to carry out his plan to betray Jesus.*

3 Jesus knew that the Father had given him authority over everything and that he had come from God and would return to God.

4 So he got up from the table, took off his robe, wrapped a towel around his waist,

5 and poured water into a basin. Then he began to wash the disciples' feet and to wipe them with the towel he had around him.

6 When he came to Simon Peter, Peter said to him, "Lord, why are you going to wash my feet?"

7 Jesus replied, "You don't understand now why I am doing it; someday you will."

8 "No," Peter protested, "you will never wash my feet!" Jesus replied, "But if I don't wash you, you won't belong to me."

9 Simon Peter exclaimed, "Then wash my hands and head as well, Lord, not just my feet!"

DO I HAVE TO BECOME A "MARTYR?"

If it's for Jesus, it's ok. When we look at the "heroes of the faith," we can hardly complain!

Hebrews 11:38-12:1 (NLT) *"They were too good for this world. They wandered over deserts and mountains, hiding in caves and holes in the ground.*

39 All of these people we have mentioned received God's approval because of their faith, yet none of them received all that God had promised.

40 For God had far better things in mind for us that would also benefit them, for they can't receive the prize at the end of the race until we finish the race.

1 Therefore, since we are surrounded by such a huge crowd of witnesses to the life of faith, let us strip off every weight that slows us down, especially the sin that so easily hinders our progress. And let us run with endurance the race that God has set before us."

IS LEGALISM ONE OF THE GREATEST HINDRANCES TO PURE RELIGION?

Legalism, to me, just has a negative ring to it. And, we see in the teachings of Jesus how much **He despised those who could quote Scripture and prove how spiritual they were, while neglecting others' needs, including their own families**. You hardly, if ever, see a legalist going out of their way to help someone, unless it benefits them even more. The following Bible passages tell just how important our lives and our examples are to people in the world today.

2 Corinthians 3:2-3; 6 (NIV) *"You yourselves are our letter, written on our hearts, known and read by everybody.*

3 You show that you are a letter from Christ, the result of our ministry, written not with ink but with the Spirit of the living God, not on tablets of stone but on tablets of human hearts."

2 Corinthians 3:6 (NIV) "He has made us competent as ministers of a new covenant— not of the letter but of the Spirit; <u>for the letter kills, but the Spirit gives life."</u>

What is a legalist? In Biblical terms, it usually means someone who is concerned with keeping the law, but many times uses it to judge or condemn others, rather than to help them understand the scriptures, and to help them serve God. A legalist is one who is always right, in their minds. If I am keeping the commandments, and if I know the Bible really well, that's how I know I am spiritually strong. **And yet, a legalist has no joy and no peace, always looking for faults and shortcomings in others. What a way to live!** The religious leaders in Jesus' day gave Him the most grief. They clearly had a different agenda than He did. Here's His warning to us about legalist.

Matthew 5:20 (KJV) *"For I say unto you, that except your righteousness shall exceed the righteousness of the scribes and Pharisees, ye shall in no case enter into the kingdom of heaven."*

John 5:38-40 (NKJV) *"But you do not have His word abiding in you, because whom He sent, Him you do not believe.*

39 "You search the Scriptures, for in them you think you have eternal life; and these are they which testify of Me.

40 "But you are not willing to come to Me that you may have life."

WAS THERE SOMETHING SPECIAL ABOUT THEM?

Them being the new converts we see in the book of Acts, following the day of Pentecost. This was a very positive, upbeat group of people. They were literally having a ball! Yes, hard times were just ahead, but they were truly living in the moment and enjoying their newfound fellowship. **Did they have a secret? It wasn't supposed to be a secret, but many people thought they were kind of crazy.** Looking at the first several chapters of Acts, we know that it was the Holy Spirit that made all the difference. The Holy Spirit would continue to lead and guide them into many wonderful, exciting exploits for Jesus. They had the filling, anointing, baptizing, cleansing, enabling, Holy Spirit within them!

The next time you feel overwhelmed, or frustrated, with life's circumstances, just look back at some of these men and women of the Bible, and be encouraged! That's what they did. They had the stories of Old Testament servants of God who survived and conquered just about everything. In Christ, we are the people of God today! He is no less interested in us and what we face on a daily basis. That make us special in His eyes!

Romans 8:37-39 (NKJV*) "Yet in all these things we are more than conquerors through Him who loved us.*

38 For I am persuaded that neither death nor life, nor angels nor principalities nor powers, nor things present nor things to come,

39 nor height nor depth, nor any other created thing, shall be able to separate us from the love of God which is in Christ Jesus our Lord."

WON'T IT BE WONDERFUL IN HEAVEN?

It's so true: when we die to self, we will live forever in heaven. No cost will be too great! Jesus' own example is well versed in this old hymn:

"I gave My life for thee, My precious blood I shed,

'That thou might'st ransomed be,

And quickened from the dead;

I gave, I gave My life for thee

What hast thou giv'n for Me?

I gave, I gave My life for thee

What hast thou giv'n for Me?

.... Frances R. Havergal....Philip P. Bliss

Revelation 12:10-11 (NIV) *Then I heard a loud voice in heaven say: "Now have come the salvation and the power and the kingdom of our God, and the authority of his Christ. For the accuser of our*

brothers, who accuses them before our God Day and night, has been hurled down.

11 They overcame him by the blood of the Lamb and by the word of their testimony; _they did not love their lives so much as to shrink from death._

We are Your people, Lord. Thank You for including each one of us in Your kingdom, and Your kingdom work. May we truly understand that the "Essence of Pure Religion" is just being Jesus every day. In His Name. Amen

SOMETHING TO THINK ABOUT:

In your own words, how would you describe the "Essence of Pure Religion?

CHAPTER 20

DOES <u>MY</u> LEGACY EVEN MATTER?

Philippians 1:6 (KJV)
Being confident of this very thing, that he which hath begun a good work in you will perform it until the day of Jesus Christ.

HAVE YOU EVER FELT LIKE A MOLDOVIAN MONK!

I have. Julia, our local Christian tour guide, led our WMA mission group out of the city to a rural area, en route to visit a monastery. We had to get off the bus in order to get to the top of a mountain, a very steep foot walk of about a quarter of a mile. Near the top of the hill, a cave faces outward in the side of the cliff where a Monk lived. On our way back down, we went into the back entrance to his living quarters, going several hundred feet through a tunnel to where he had been living for several years. He believed that he could most impact the world by being nearer to God, alone and praying, instead of living what most of us would consider a "normal" life. His (open) front entrance had an immediate drop off of hundreds of feet, and there was no barrier. It was a beautiful view of the majestic valley below. It was very serene**. It seemed like a perfect place to get away from everything, the busyness and cares of a very troubled world, if one were to decide, as a Christian, to live a life separated from the world below.**

Our small group of about a dozen included several teenagers. We admired his "quarters," which included a gift shop, and a very narrow bedroom just a few feet from his, cliff-side, front door. Some of us wanted to hear a "word," from what we perceived as a very spiritual man of God, a message from God, that would encourage us. **So, we asked him, "Do you have anything you would like to say to us before we leave?" "Yes," he said, "please don't chew gum in here!"** I have always wondered why that would be his first words in answer to our questioning him about something spiritual. It could be that some of the teenagers in our group had already been chewing gum inside his residence. I also think that, with so many tour groups coming to his cave, he was being exposed to more of the world than he had anticipated or cared for.

DOES GOD HAVE A SPECIFIC PLAN FOR EACH OF US?

It usually takes a lifetime for most of us to begin to see what God had planned for us all along. I think that if I had been more aware of God's plan for my life, as a young boy, He might have fulfilled His plan in me much sooner. Yes, there actually were times when, **like that Moldovian Monk, that I thought about just staying in the mountains, moving even farther back into the hills, to enjoy my serenity and find my pleasure in being with the wild animals. Who could that hurt?**

However, because God is God, and has a specific plan for each one of us, He doesn't allow us to simply escape, unless we actually believe it's His plan for us. As I have said earlier, "I love my solitude, but I desperately need people in my life!" So, he puts in my heart, not only the desire to serve Him, His way, He also puts within me the ability to do so: **"For God is working in you, giving you the desire to obey him and the power to do what pleases him."**

Philippians 2:13 (NLT)

FOR ME, IT ALL STARTED AT THE BEGINNING!

I was born the last of eleven children to **Cecil William Sr and Emily Todd.** Although we were very poor, we were blessed beyond measure. For me, I was especially blessed in having eight siblings who were all mentors to me. I thank God for every one of them. I have so many special thoughts and memories of each one as I recall things that happened, which have helped me throughout my entire life. Of course, we had our times of disagreements, arguments, and disappointments. **When I was in the recording studio recording the song, "The Good Times We Had," my brother, Bob, was also in the studio, listening, and said to me, jokingly, "did we grow up in the same place?"** All the basic tenets that I needed to know would come through my eight brothers and two sisters, while not overlooking my parents who cared for all of us very much. **As I look back, it is with a grateful heart that I say, "Thank you, T. R.; Bill; June; John D; Bob; Cecil; Harry; Lee; Grady; and Josie. I believe we'll all be together again in heaven. Can't wait!"**

While my brothers and sisters were a blessing to me, it then was up to me, alone, to go to work and put into practice what I had learned, including my spiritual life. One of the greatest things in life, for me, has been to realize God's plan and purpose for my life. I love sharing and teaching this concept wherever I go: to juveniles; the homeless; prisoners; or, to foreigners. I agree with the apostle Paul: *"For to me, to live is Christ, and to die is gain."* **Philippians 1:21 (NKJV)** I am also very much aware that it's not me! It's Jesus in me! Left to myself, my life would have meant nothing. I would have "self-imploded" very quickly.

GOD HAD TO TEAR OUT <u>MY</u> HEART!

"I know that nothing good lives in me, that is, in my sinful nature. For I have the desire to do what is good, but I cannot carry it out." **Romans 7:18 (NIV)**

"I will give you a new heart and put a new spirit within you; I will take the heart of stone out of your flesh and give you a heart of flesh.

27 "I will put My Spirit within you and cause you to walk in My statutes, and you will keep My judgments and do them." **Ezekiel 36:26-27 (NKJV)**

I am convinced that I would never have realized what God wanted to do in me, until I knew what He wanted <u>from me.</u> God wanted, and still wants, all of me. I would like to encourage you to pray earnestly, every day, to know what God wants from you, so that He can do what He is wanting to do through you. This doesn't mean to do nothing until you understand everything. Rather, it means that He is wanting to work in you, and through you, moment by moment, to accomplish His will. **<u>Every day: surrender your heart/desires; your mind/thoughts; your body/a living sacrifice and a temple of the Holy Spirit; your soul/your deepest inner being; and your spirit, to the indwelling and control of the Holy Spirit.</u>** That's the only way we can successfully accomplish God's great work.

"Father, let the Holy Ghost have full dominion over me, in my home, in my temper, in every word of my tongue, in every thought of my heart, in every feeling toward my fellow men; Let the Holy Spirit have entire possession." **...Andrew Murray - Daily Thoughts on Holiness.**

WHAT'S YOUR STORY?

One of the reasons I like to look back is that I believe God made each of us in His image to show his great love through our circumstances. Would we have chosen a different story than what He gave us? our color, our country, our looks, or our talents, abilities, and skills? **Perhaps the reason He put each one of us where are was to bring glory to Him, not ourselves.** Has He not been with us every step of the way? What, then, is the purpose of our circumstances, successes, and failures, if not for a much greater purpose, an eternal purpose, that He has already prepared for us.

For me, it is to remind myself that the Lord, Jesus, is always with me. He picks me up when I stumble and fall. He loves me, no matter what. He invites me to walk with Him every day, and to see Him in every circumstance. **He is the one who took me to Zambia, where I observed, firsthand, the plight of orphans and widows, then, through the Holy Spirit, challenged me to do something about it.** I promised that I would be obedient. immediately, the idea of writing a book, called: "Pure Religion," came to me.

I said to the Lord, "If you want me to do this, it must be from You, totally!" I also prayed, "Lord, use this to bring relief to orphans and widows around the world. "I even pictured an ever-extending ministry, a world hunger project, "Feeding both body and soul:" The Word of God for the soul, and bread for the hungry." Who would like to join me in this project?

"Only one life, will soon be past;

Only what's done for Christ will last.

Dear God, thank you for putting your Spirit and Your desires in me, and for challenging me to surrender everything to You, day-by-day. May I become more and more like Jesus. In His Name. Amen.

SOMETHING TO THINK ABOUT:

How am I becoming more like Jesus?

Printed in the USA
CPSIA information can be obtained
at www.ICGtesting.com
JSHW080837200324
59526JS00006B/34

9 781962 142106